San

Lane Publishing Co.

Francisco

A Sunset Pictorial

San Francisco

by the EDITORS of SUNSET BOOKS and SUNSET MAGAZINE

EDITED BY JACK MCDOWELL

REVISED EDITION Edited by Dorothy Krell

DESIGN AND GRAPHICS COORDINATION: William Gibson, Joe Seney

CARTOGRAPHY: Phillip Willette

ILLUSTRATIONS: Gordon Brusstar

EDITORIAL ASSISTANTS: Elizabeth Hogan, Mary Benton Smith

SPECIAL CONSULTANTS: George Knight, American Society of
Magazine Photographers
Richard Dillon, Sutro Library

PHOTOGRAPHS

ANSEL ADAMS: 17; 42 (all courtesy Redwood Empire Association). JOHN ARMS: 171 bottom; 202 top. BANCROFT LIBRARY: 19; 21 bottom; 23 bottom; 27; 34; 35. BANK OF AMERICA: 153 bottom right. BAY AREA RAPID TRANSIT: 146; 251. SUELLEN BILOW-LERCH: 134 right; 135; 156 top; 160; 162; 247 top. LEE BLODGETT: 8; 9; 11; 159 top. RICHARD BROOKS: 167; 177 bottom. MICHAEL BRY: 85; 96 top; 123 top; 126 top right; 182 right; 187. CALIFORNIA HISTORICAL SOCIETY: 29; 37. NICK CARTER: 10; 124; 125; 128; 236. WILLIAM CARTER: 91 right; 108; 208; 220 top. GLENN CHRISTIANSEN: 81 top right; 170 top right; 197; 199; 203 top; 207 left; 213 top; 216 right. FRAN COLEBERD: 18; 104 right; 144. ROBERT COX: 133. MADISON DEVLIN: 47; 103; 178; 180; 188; 249 top. ROGER FLANAGAN: 88 bottom left; 245 top, bottom; 247. LEE FOSTER: 203 bottom. GERALD R. FREDRICK: 72 left; 114 bottom; 170 bottom right; 171 top, 200, 202 center. PETER FRONK: 69; 79 center, bottom; 94; 95; 118 right; 149; 161; 186 top; 191 top, center; 235 top. GOLDEN GATE BRIDGE: 240 top. DAVE HARTLEY: 189. MIKE HAYDEN: 195 top. EDWIN HOFFMAN: 50 bottom. BOB HOLLINGSWORTH: 107 top; 121; 140; 206 bottom; 207 left; 228; 229; 230. ROBERT ISAACS: 82 top right; 127; 132; 233; 243. PIRKLE JONES: 129 bottom. GEORGE KNIGHT: 38 top; 81 bottom; 93; 99; 104; 122; 145; 168 top; 174 bottom; 246 top. DOROTHY KRELL: 88 bottom right. ROY KRELL: 214. HOLGER KREUZHAGE: 183. JOHN LARSEN: 75; 185; 194; 226 left. LIBRARY OF CONGRESS: 21 top. ELLS MARUGG: 148 bottom; 152; 202 bottom. ELAINE MAYES: 147 top. MIKE MCCURRY: 96 bottom; 123 bottom; 142 top; 163; 206 top. JACK MCDOWELL: 25; 26; 78 bottom; 81 top left; 88 top; 100 bottom; 109 bottom; 111; 113 bottom; 116; 118 left; 119; 130 top; 131; 141 top right, bottom; 142 bottom; 143 top right; 147 bottom; 151; 159 bottom; 164 left; 165 bottom right; 170 left; 179; 192; 195 bottom; 201; 205; 209; 211 bottom; 212; 213 bottom; 215; 221 bottom; 223; 239; 248; 249 bottom. WILLIAM MCKINNEY: 172; PHIZ MOZESSON: 109 top. DAVID MUENCH: 106; 154–155. TOM MYERS: 91 left; 129 top. PATRICK O'ROURKE: 62. PACIFIC FAR EAST LINE: 156 bottom. PACIFIC GAS & ELECTRIC: 220 bottom; 222. PHIL PALMER: 98; 104 left; 137; 181. PETE REDPATH: 245 center. PIONEER SOCIETY OF CALIFORNIA: 20; 23 top; 30 bottom; 33; 41; 45; 55. NORMAN A. PLATE: front cover; 105; 114 top; 115 top; 217; 219. BIL PLUMMER: 76 top; 80 bottom; 82 left, bottom right; 101; 153 top; 174 top; 175 top; 176; 246 bottom. WALLACE PONTIUS: 221 top. REDWOOD EMPIRE ASSOCIATION: 22; 143 left; 242. JOHN REGISTER: 80 top. KARL RIEK: 148 top. MARTHA ROSMAN: 130 bottom. HAL ROTH: 92. RICHARD ROWAN: 71; 76 bottom; 186 bottom; 190; 191 bottom; 193 bottom; 244. SAN FRANCISCO CHAMBER OF COMMERCE: 61; 216 left. SAN FRANCISCO CONVENTION & VISITORS BUREAU: 177 top; 182 left; 198; 210; 225 right. SAN FRANCISCO PRESIDIO: 30 top; 31 bottom. NORMAN PRINCE: 112 bottom; 113 top. SAN FRANCISCO PUBLIC UTILITIES COMMISSION: 252; 253. SHERATON-PALACE HOTEL: 60. SMITHSONIAN INSTITUTION: 38; 48; 51. SOUTHERN PACIFIC: 46 top; 53; 54 top; 56 left, right; 57; 58; 59 bottom left, bottom center left, bottom right; 107 bottom. W. D. A. STEPHENS: 110 right. LEVI STRAUSS & CO.: 49. TOM TRACY: 1–2; 6–7; 70; 74; 78 top; 83; 86–87; 97; 117; 196; 218; 224; 234; 235 bottom; 238. TEDDY TSOI: 90 bottom; 126 top left, bottom. UNION PACIFIC RAILROAD MUSEUM COLLECTION: 56 center. U.S. ARMY SIGNAL CORPS: 240 bottom; MCLEOD VOLZ: 112 top. DARROW M. WATT: 203 center; 157. CHARLES WECKLER: back cover. WELLS FARGO BANK HISTORY ROOM: 36; 39; 40; 43; 46 bottom; 50 top; 52; 54 bottom; 59 top, bottom center right; 63; 153 bottom left; bottom center left; bottom center right; 173; 193 top. PETER O. WHITELEY: 72 right. BARON WOLMAN: 139. GEORGE WOO: 90 top; 164 right; 165 left, top right; 237. NATHAN ZABARSKY: 241. NIKOLAY ZUREK: 31 top; 100 top; 106 top; 110 left; 138; 141 top left; 143 center right, bottom right; 168 bottom; 169; 175 bottom; 211 top; 225 left; 226 right. CRAIG ZWICKY: 115 bottom.

FRONT COVER: Victorians and downtown skyline from Alamo Square. Photograph by Norman A. Plate.

Executive Editor, Sunset Books: David E. Clark

First Printing March 1977

Contents

San Francisco—a peninsular city, formed through the forces of

a capricious sea, a restless bay, and a benevolent climate.

A clean, white city, shaped by the timeless energies of nature and the tireless exuberance of man—a city whose independent spirit is fostered by its physical isolation, whose variety derives from the character of the people attracted to its shores.

A compact city, whose structures thrust boldly toward the clouds, whose residents respect the past and savor the present while stepping with unhurried confidence toward the future.

11

*The city's cradle days were calm,
quiet—and relatively short-lived. With the
discovery of gold, San Francisco
entered its brawling youth. By the time
of the silver boom, some of
the rough edges were beginning to wear off.
But only after its partial destruction
did the city settle down
to maturity and honest self-respect.*

BEGINNINGS OF A BOOM TOWN

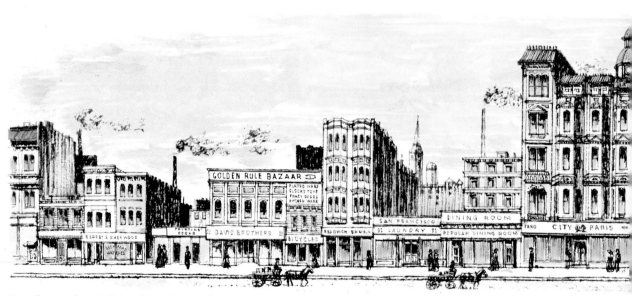

Retail row, about 1894—Geary Street, between Kearny and Stockton.

THE DISCOVERY of what today is San Francisco was an ironic accident, a twist of fate that started a pattern of fitful boom and bust that characterized the place for decades to follow.

By the middle of the eighteenth century, Spanish treasure galleons and ships of exploration had been voyaging up and down the California coast for well over two hundred years. The mariners were prudent enough to stay well off the unknown and rugged shoreline, but in so doing they time and time again sailed past a narrow inlet beyond which lay a gigantic natural harbor. In 1769 a land expedition led by Don Gaspar de Portola was sent out from Mexico to extend Spanish colonization in what seemed a territory of great promise—Alta California. The party's target was Monterey, where a settlement had already been established, and on the way north it kept near the coast except when forced by mountains or other natural obstacles to turn inland. One such barrier caused the expedition to detour shortly before it would have reached Monterey. Several days later the travel-weary Portola found his way blocked by a large and unidentifiable body of water—the bay of San Francisco. Rather than feeling any proprietory right in the discovery, Portola was bitterly disappointed at having missed his objective.

By the late 1700's Spain was becoming increasingly concerned over the possibility of Russia putting colonists into California, and the Viceroy at Mexico City sent the ship *San Carlos* north, instructing Captain Manuel de

Ayala to survey the enigmatic Gulf of the Farallones. In August, 1775, Ayala anchored within the Golden Gate, proving at least to his satisfaction that the bay chronicled earlier actually existed and could support a colony. The following year Captain Juan Bautista de Anza brought a group of settlers, priests, and soldiers, who established a mission and military garrison as a first step in extending the empire of Spain.

Unfortunately, the colonizing influence of the California missions was negated in 1833 by the Secularization Act, which took away local church powers and caused mission property to fall to government appointed administrators, many of whom were concerned more with swelling their personal holdings than with furthering the influence of Mexico. In a short time Yerba Buena—the tiny village by the big bay—was known only to the few persons who lived there.

Though Mexico had apparently forgotten its northernmost territory, the rest of the world hadn't. England and several other countries were making furtive moves toward California when on July 9, 1846, the American naval Captain, John B. Montgomery, boldly raised the stars and stripes over Yerba Buena.

Under the influence of enterprising Yankees, San Francisco enjoyed a surge of popularity which settled down to slow yet steady growth. Its founding fathers—merchants such as William Richardson, Jacob Leese, Thomas Larkin, W. D. M. Howard, Sam Brannan—were far-sighted men who could sense the potential of the place but who were content to use their native in-

Insurance alley, about 1900—Montgomery Street, between California and Sutter.

San Francisco...a new frenzy

genuity in developing it and their fortunes. San Francisco was on its quiet way to becoming a respectable town when in 1848 fate intervened in the form of gold.

San Francisco became a boom town as well as a ghost town virtually overnight. Though a tide of men poured into the place from all over the world, most stayed no longer than it took to get outfitted and book passage to the diggings. When the gold fever finally died down, San Francisco was forced to find new ways to prop up a sagging economy. Agriculture and world trade seemed one answer, and then as the place was adjusting to a steady, hardworking respectability, fate moved again in the 1860's with the discovery of an unbelievably rich mountain of silver in Nevada.

Though the source of the riches was in another state, the men who knew how to exploit it were not. John Mackay, James Fair, William O'Brien, and James Flood were four perceptive individuals who became fabulously wealthy by controlling the heaviest producing mines in the Comstock, and they started a new frenzy in San Francisco that was all wrapped up in silver, high finance, and railroads.

Completion of the transcontinental railroad brought the city to greater ferment and created a fresh crop of millionaires, among which were Mark Hopkins, Collis Huntington, Leland Stanford, and Charles Crocker.

But millionaires and tumult both tend to fade away, and when the city was once more on its way up from an economic slump, Nature took a hand and the whole place came down in ruins.

1542-1776:

A Frontier
Ripe for Conquest

The aggressive Conquistadores had much of the Americas under their control by the middle of the sixteenth century and were casting covetous eyes to the north for new lands to acquire for their king. In 1542 the Viceroy of Mexico commissioned a Portuguese seafarer named Juan Rodriguez Cabrillo to find a northwest passage from the Atlantic to the Pacific and to explore the west coast of North America. Cabrillo landed briefly at the present site of San Diego Bay, then continued north, passing what is now San Francisco Bay. After Cabrillo's death on the return trip south, Bartolome Ferrelo took command and once more drove the ships up the coast, this time going as far as Oregon before being forced back by stormy seas. Although Ferrelo came within seeing range of the Golden Gate four times in all, he was unaware of its existence.

For over two hundred years mariners coursed north and swept south along the California coast, but none seems to have realized that he was passing the entrance to one of the world's greatest natural harbors.

TIMELESS AND UNCHANGING, the rugged coast of upper California in many places looks just as it did some four hundred years ago, when Cabrillo, Cermeno, Vizcaino, and others struck north from Mexico looking for new lands to claim for the Spanish crown.

SPANIARDS, PORTUGUESE, and a most elusive body of water

FREQUENT FOGS, rocky shores, and a ragged, irregular coastline all conspired to conceal the narrow entrance to San Francisco Bay from the eyes of Spanish and Portuguese mariners who sailed up and down California. Though several seagoing explorers passed close to the Farallon Islands between 1500 and 1700—some even stopping there—none seem to have been aware of the break in the shoreline only 30 miles to the east.

IT WAS BY ACCIDENT that San Francisco Bay was discovered. In November of 1769, Gaspar de Portola and his land expedition were looking for the bay of Monterey; overshooting it, they continued north until stopped by a great inland reach of water north of Montara Mountain.

Some Just Sailed on By

For more than 200 years of recorded history, voyagers—seeking a northern strait, new lands, perhaps the legendary "Lost Port" of the Spanish conquistadores—sailed up and down the Alta California coast without discovering the great but hidden inner bay of San Francisco.

Juan Rodriguez Cabrillo set sail from Mexico on June 27, 1542, and explored the Pacific Coast of Baja California. The Portuguese navigator continued up the Alta California coast and reported a "great gulf" (possibly directly opposite the Golden Gate). He was driven back down the coast by severe storms.

Bartolome Ferrelo, Cabrillo's chief pilot, left the Channel Islands February 22, 1543, after Cabrillo's death, and once more worked his way north; he charted the Farallon Islands and twice passed by the bay's entrance.

Francis Drake, English navigator and admiral, landed near latitude 38°, just a few miles above San Francisco, on June 17, 1579. He spent six weeks on the Alta California coast and annexed the land to England under the name "Nova Albion."

Sebastian Rodriguez Cermeno, Spanish army captain, left Manila and reached the Alta California coast on November 4, 1595. Three days later he took possession of the coast and gave the name of San Francisco to what is now Drake's Bay.

Sebastian Vizcaino, Basque explorer and merchant, sailed from Acapulco in May, 1602, passed probably within sight of the big bay, and went as far north as Cape Mendocino.

Not until over 150 years later was the first sighting recorded. During Gaspar de Portola's 1769 land expedition, his chief scout, Jose Francisco de Ortega, reported seeing the southern arm of the bay. Portola himself viewed the bay but was unaware of his discovery.

It wasn't until 1775 that a ship was known to have entered the bay. On August 5, Spanish Navy Lieutenant Juan Manuel de Ayala passed through the Golden Gate aboard the *San Carlos*. His was the first ship into San Francisco Bay.

...AN ELUSIVE BODY OF WATER

SAN CARLOS, the supply ship dispatched from Monterey to meet Anza's colonists from Mexico, was two months at sea on her passage up the coast. The ship was the first vessel known to have entered San Francisco Bay.

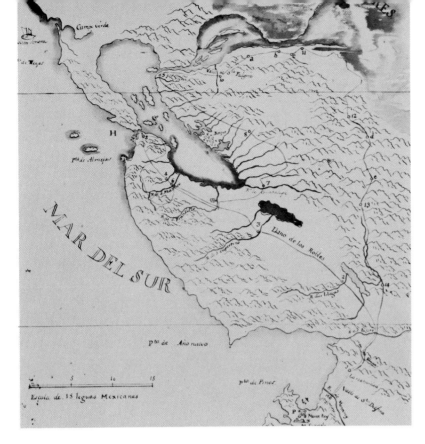

SAN FRANCISCO BAY, as mapped by Father Pedro Font in 1776. Route marked around area was taken by Font, Moraga, and Anza after fulfilling their prime objective of setting up two crosses, one at the location of the future presidio, the other at the place the mission was to be built.

REMARKABLE fortitude was exhibited by Juan Bautista de Anza and his party of settlers, who for three months struggled through the wilderness from Mexico to Monterey. Anza and a small group continued north to establish the sites for the future presidio and mission (see map above).

THE VENERABLE plate of brass – historical fact or comfortable legend?

POINT REYES, named in honor of the "day of the Three Kings," lies 40 miles north of San Francisco. Sir Francis Drake—terror of Spanish shipping in the 1570's—is believed to have repaired his vessel, the Golden Hinde, in the small bay near the top of the picture.

SIR FRANCIS DRAKE, English gentleman, master mariner, plunderer of Spanish treasure ships that plied the Pacific —yet an enigma to modern scholars, who cannot agree whether he was a sophisticated pirate or a man with a secret mission from his Queen. It was Drake's presence in the western Pacific that alarmed the Spanish into developing California.

REMARKABLE relic, this inscribed plate of brass claiming English possession of California and naming it Nova Albion is believed to have been left by Drake in 1579. Found in Marin County in the 1930's, the plate forms a thrilling display at the Bancroft Library at the University of California in Berkeley.

1776-1825:

The Mission and the Military

AS PART OF THEIR EFFORTS to colonize the New World in the name of the Crown and God, the Spanish set up a series of missions that stretched from the southern half of Baja California to the northern half of Alta California. The purpose of the missions was twofold: to Christianize the heathen Indian, and to act as a nucleus for further colonization by Spain. In conjunction with establishment of a mission, a military garrison was often set up as a show of force to anyone else who might have designs on the land.

San Francisco de Asis was the sixth mission in the California chain, founded in 1776 on a peninsula of land that separated the Pacific Ocean from the port that was reported to be large enough to hold all the ships of Imperial Spain. Not far from the mission, on a strategic promontory where ostensibly it could protect the harbor entrance, was the presidio or fort. In spite of noble aims, both mission and presidio fell into decline, and early in the 1800's they became little more than deteriorating outposts within a neglected settlement.

CIVIL AND MILITARY authority was combined in the delicate office of Gobernador. Don Luis Antonio Arguello was the first appointed Mexican Governor of California, holding office from 1823 to 1825. His grave is surrounded by an iron fence in a shaded corner of Mission Dolores cemetery, adjacent to the original mission building.

THE CHURCH by the lake of sorrows

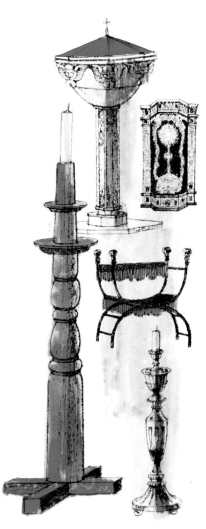

"*IF SAINT FRANCIS desires a mission, let him show us his harbor and he shall have one,*" Inspector-General Galvez told Serra when they were planning Alta California missions. Original name of "St. Francis de Asis" given mission by founder, Father Francisco Palou, was gradually replaced by "Dolores," taken after a nearby lake. In settling the missions, pursuant to establishment of a Spanish colony, one of the first steps was to urge local natives to embrace Christianity. The large wooden candlestick in the drawing of mission details at left was made by local Indians. Below, Indian men dance after Sunday service while priests look on.

CALIFORNIA'S presiding missionary, Father Junipero Serra (opposite page), was insistent on a mission being founded in honor of Saint Francis. Statue of this dedicated man stands in Mission Dolores cemetery.

"SEVERAL HUTS on the waterside...the men go quite naked"

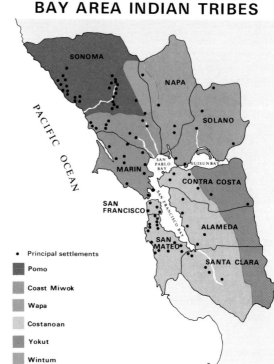

- Principal settlements
- ▮ Pomo
- ▮ Coast Miwok
- ▮ Wapa
- ▮ Costanoan
- ▮ Yokut
- ▮ Wintum

TENACIOUS of land rights, the bay region's early Indian tribes kept within sharply delineated territories, their settlements usually strung out along water.

Indians-Earliest Residents of the Bay

Before the white man, the bay region's inhabitants were the California Indians. Enjoying a gentle climate, a sea full of fish, and a year-round harvest—and without the hardships of most American Indians—they languished in a comparatively under-developed Indian culture.

Generally, each tribe lived in small, close-knit tribelets, each speaking a different version of one linguistic family, the Penutian. Their dwellings were dome-shaped structures made from sticks, brush, and reeds. Usually men went naked and women wore loose-hanging skirts of deerskin, tule, or bark fiber; both adorned their faces and breasts with tattoos. Except for the chiefs, monogamy was the general rule. A man would buy his bride with strings of thin shell discs, then live with his wife's people. They speared fish from tule rafts and hunted game with bow and arrow. Acorns were the staple for many, and wild seeds, roots, berries, and greens completed an unusually well-rounded diet. Only the Yokuts made pots; most squaws cooked in watertight baskets and carried their babies in tule cradles.

Before aliens forced their civilization upon the Indians, explorers brought back sympathetic reports. Francis Drake noted in 1579 that the Miwoks handled their bows and arrows "very skillfully" and ran "very swiftly, and long." Father Crespi in 1772 called the Costanoans friendly, and observed that they were "redheaded, bearded, and fair."

WITH THE FOUNDING of the mission, the lot of local Indians improved somewhat, since they were fed, housed, and clothed. This sketch of the presidio (made in 1816 by Louis Choris, a visiting artist) would at first glance seem to indicate a master-slave relationship, but from the free conversation of the group around the fire, the horsemen were probably merely accompanying their Indian charges to the mission or to work in the fields. Native families also had plots of land assigned to them, on which they cultivated melons, fruit trees, and berries.

A MILITARY GARRISON more in name than in fact

CALIFORNIA'S northernmost military garrison was for a long while an outpost in every sense of the word. Established in 1776 (along with Mission Dolores), the presidio was never staffed by more than a handful of Mexican soldiers, and even these few depended on the mission for food. In 1826 the English explorer Captain Frederick Beechey, who entered San Francisco Bay on a mapping expedition, was appalled by the neglect into which the place had fallen. Its fortifications were three rusty cannons that served mainly to prop up a half-dressed sentry. Above, the presidio in slightly better days, in 1806; below, in 1853, after being garrisoned and spruced up by American soldiers.

MAIN PURPOSE of the presidio has been defense of the Golden Gate, though over the years it has gained distinction as the largest military reserve in any United States city, containing a fort, a parade ground, a hospital, an airfield. Headstones in its national military cemetery date back to the 1700's.

SPANISH AMERICAN WAR, in 1898, brought troops and transport ships. Alcatraz was occupied by Coast Artillery detachments and was used as a disciplinary barracks.

1825-1848:

Yankees are a Wonderful People

DURING THE EARLY 1800's the shoreside settlement on San Francisco Bay was literally forgotten by the authorities in Mexico City. There was little communication between it and Monterey, capital of Alta California, and practically none with Mexico. The colonists considered themselves chiefly ranchers and between fiestas made the best of their idle time with such diversions as pitting bulls against bears or snatching roosters off the ground while riding by at full gallop.

By the 1830's the place was becoming an international roadstead, a regular port of call for New England whalers, Russian fur hunters, Yankee hide collectors, and English mappers. Sensing that the expanding maritime traffic was but a prelude to greater things, several Eastern-born merchants set up trading posts in town.

With the outbreak of war between Mexico and the United States in the spring of 1846, the Americans moved quickly in California. In June an attempt was made by a band of Yankees to overthrow the Mexicans in Northern California, and they succeeded in establishing the dubious "California Republic" at Sonoma. Early in July Monterey was formally occupied, and almost simultaneously a naval detachment dropped anchor off Yerba Buena. After landing a party of soldiers and marines, the officer in charge ceremoniously raised the Stars and Stripes, thereby proclaiming the village a possession of the United States.

FANCIFUL ROMANTIC scene of San Francisco in the mid-1800's shows a virtual land of milk and honey. The happy peasants—described as "a group of Mexicans"—could have been lifted straight out of France, which they probably were, since the lithograph was done in Paris.

THE STARS AND STRIPES brought an end to a dozing outpost

AMUSEMENTS for Californians during the early 1800's were lively and characteristic of their exuberant spirit. Picture above shows the popular sport of snatching a buried rooster by the head at full gallop. At right, a bull and a bear are pitted against each other in one of the battles that were "the everlasting topics of conversation with the Californians."

YERBA BUENA, a distant settlement in Alta California, was virtually ignored by the authorities in Mexico City for decades. By the early 1800's the mission (above) was crumbling from neglect, the Indian population had been thinned out drastically by illness introduced by the white man, the presidio was "little better than a heap of rubbish and bones, on which jackals, dogs, and vultures were constantly preying." It was a time of discontent, a time ripe for change.

...END OF AN OUTPOST

THE STARS AND STRIPES flies over Yerba Buena! In 1835 the United States offered
Mexico $500,000 for the northern half of California, to no avail. The world had its eyes on the
American west, and England was believed to be negotiating for the province (an Irish priest
was even raising funds to bring a group of Catholic colonists over). On July 9, 1846, less than
a month after American John C. Fremont's abortive Bear Flag revolt, Commander J. B.
Montgomery arrived in the USS Portsmouth and raised the American flag.

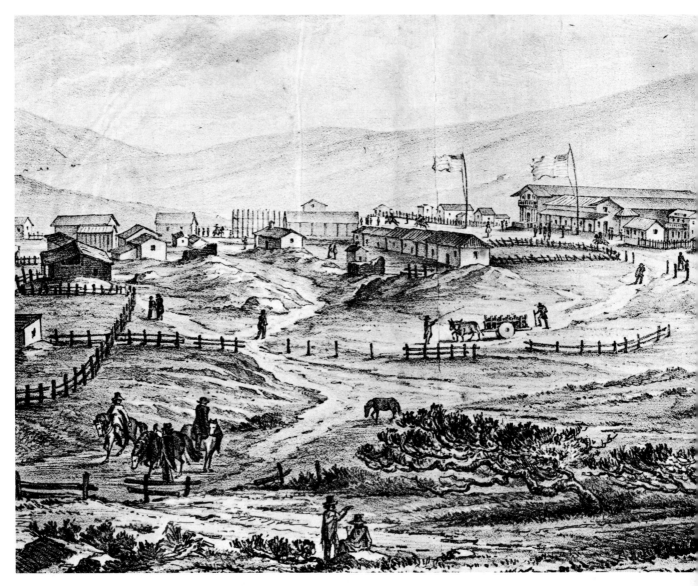

AMERICAN FLAGS wave proudly in a stiff breeze. Shortly after California became part of the United States, newcomers headed into the state from other parts of the country. Most of the residents of Yerba Buena were Americans and Spanish Californians; there were also a few Europeans and New Zealanders. With such a mixed, growing population, activities expanded from the center of town in Portsmouth Plaza out to the mission district.

UNKNOWN ARTISTS of the time depicted San Francisco in mid-1800's. Painting above (which hangs in the fascinating History Room of Wells Fargo Bank) shows the bay lapping at the foot of Telegraph Hill, which is dotted with gold seekers' temporary tents. Picture of Yerba Buena at left was probably made before Gold Rush, judging from the pastoral quality of village and peaceful appearance of the waterfront.

"ONE RESTAURANT...two grog shops ...a blacksmith"

KEARNY AND CLAY, before the middle of the nineteenth century, was already a part of the town's center. The popular City Hotel was originally the store and home of William Leidesdorff, a pioneer business man from the West Indies who became American Vice-Consul under Mexican rule. A French visitor of the time commented that the houses scattered along the shore and on the hill behind the hotel belonged to "foreigners."

...GROWTH OF A VILLAGE

EARLY HAZARDS included mud deep enough to swallow men as well as wagons and pack animals. At one time merchants sank bags of flour, cotton bales, and uncrated cook stoves for a foundation from which they hawked their wares standing. Board walks that were built on the mire became in effect floating bridges.

PORTSMOUTH PLAZA in the mid-1800's bustled with frenzied activity stemming from Gold Rush, and it seemed that the town was here to stay. When mail arrived once a month at the post-office (tall building at far left), lines of waiting men stretched from Clay Street to beyond Sacramento. Building in center is the Justice's Court; on right is the old adobe custom house; in foreground is the horse market. The other sides of the plaza were lined with boisterous gambling halls and amusement houses, where miners who were lucky enough to bring gold dust back from the diggings could part with it with very little effort.

SURE SIGN of growth was the appearance of steamers on the bay. In 1847 William Leidesdorff brought a small boat from Alaska, called—for want of a better name—"The Steamboat." With the discovery of gold, several steamers were shipped in pieces from the Eastern United States and assembled in San Francisco to carry cargo and passengers up the Sacramento and San Joaquin Rivers. Cabin passage to Sacramento was $30, plus $5 if the berth was used.

WHALERS AND TRADERS – the
start of a great maritime trade

YERBA BUENA, original name given to San Francisco, was taken from the mint that grew wild over dunes in the area. The village was a stopping-over place for Russian traders in sea otter fur, who established Fort Ross 90 miles up the coast as a base of operations in California.

ABOVE: Ships waiting to be loaded or unloaded in 1837; probably some of them belonged to the Hudson's Bay Company, which maintained a trading post in Yerba Buena. The artist, John J. Vioget, was the town's first surveyor and a trencherman of renown, once putting away pancakes, stew, steak, tamales, cake, and pie at a single sitting. RIGHT: Transports, a schooner, and a merchantman anchored in Yerba Buena Cove in 1847. Montgomery Street fronts on the water, and the two streets running down to it are Clay and Washington.

1848-1906:

A Time of Wealth
...A Day of Destruction

FOR A COUPLE OF YEARS after San Francisco became a part of the United States, the village dozed on in the California sun. A few more ships came and went, a few more adventuresome souls moved in from the East, but the place remained a remote settlement, relatively untouched by commerce. At the opening of 1848 the population of San Francisco was less than 900.

By 1850, as a result of the discovery of gold in El Dorado County in the Sierra foothills, the place had grown to 56,000, a phenomenal increase of more than 55,000 people in approximately 24 months! Ships from all over the world crowded the harbor, and San Francisco became a marshaling point for one of the greatest mass movements of human beings in history.

After the gold fever cooled and the town settled down to a steady growth, a second boom occurred—the discovery of silver in Nevada. Though in an adjoining state, the bonanza wrought longer-lasting effects on San Francisco than had the discovery of gold.

At the turn of the century the city was fast becoming a sophisticated metropolis. Its adolescence was over—it was a place to be reckoned with. Then in four days, in April, 1906, the heart of San Francisco was destroyed.

SYMBOL OF AFFLUENCE, Nob Hill in the 1870's was crowned with grand mansions that were eloquent reminders to all of San Francisco of new-found wealth. At the juncture of California and Mason Streets stood the solid-as-a-rock home of James Flood; neighbors up the street were Collis Huntington (white house with big windows) and Charles Crocker.

GOLD – the sudden birth and short life of a boom town

THE PLACE WENT CRAZY! This is perhaps the best description of San Francisco in 1848-49 when anyone who could move did so in the direction of the Sierra gold fields, causing the greatest mass migration of human beings in history. Men paced the water's edge, chafing at even an hour's delay in getting transportation. The windjammer Niantic was one of several ships abandoned by passengers and crew in their rush to the diggings and later drawn up on shore to serve as hotels or stores.

46

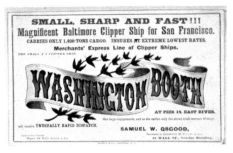

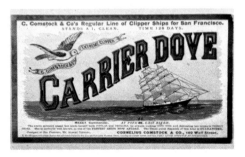

The Glorious Golden Age of Sail

*Sea Witch, Stag-Hound, Trade Wind, Flying Cloud—names that could send
a shiver of excitement down a man's spine in the mid-1800's.
These were the sleek Yankee clipper ships, built for speed, that
for two decades stormed around the Horn and boomed through the Golden
Gate, making and breaking records with every voyage. Sailing
cards as colorfully romantic as the ships they promoted
encouraged Eastern merchants to send their goods West this way.*

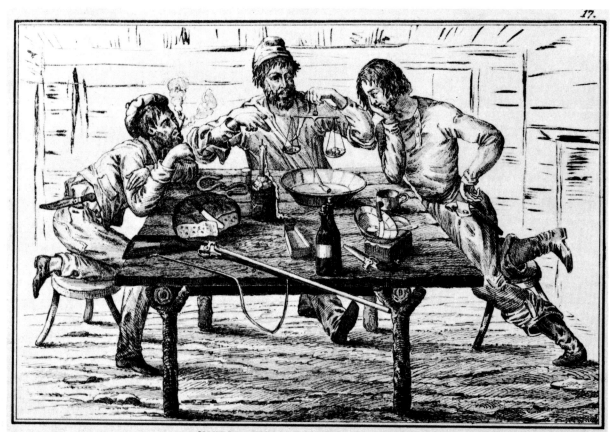

MINERS WEIGHING THEIR GOLD.

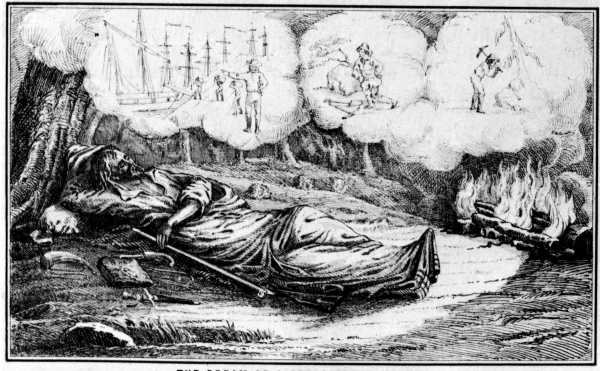

THE DREAM OF A PROSPECTING MINER.
Lith. & Published by Britton & Rey cornr. Montgomery & California Sts. S. Francisco.

...GOLD, A BOOM TOWN

LIFE AT THE MINES wasn't all it was cracked up to be, and many of the gold seekers who managed to survive came back wiser but richer only in their dreams. One sagacious argonaut—Levi Strauss—never got closer to the gold fields than San Francisco, where he prospered in making tough canvas pants for miners such as the well-attired quartet above.

A SECRET SOCIETY of respectable citizens

FREQUENT FIRES and other criminal depredations by roaming gangs of hoodlums prompted a group of citizens to organize the first Vigilance Committee in 1851 (with ubiquitous Sam Brannan as president), the second five years later. Members of the Executive Committee carried an identifying medal bearing an eye signifying that the vigilantes never slept.

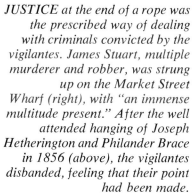

JUSTICE at the end of a rope was the prescribed way of dealing with criminals convicted by the vigilantes. James Stuart, multiple murderer and robber, was strung up on the Market Street Wharf (right), with "an immense multitude present." After the well attended hanging of Joseph Hetherington and Philander Brace in 1856 (above), the vigilantes disbanded, feeling that their point had been made.

NEVADA SILVER brought San Francisco fortunes

HEIGHTS HAD A SPECIAL APPEAL for men who dominated the economic and political life of the state. When they weren't busy downtown enlarging their fortunes, they could gaze out over the city from Nob Hill and at least in thought be master of all they surveyed. Their view to the northeast took in California Street and Yerba Buena Island.

A GREAT PART OF THE WEALTH that came out of Nevada's fabulous Comstock Lode poured into San Francisco during the late 1800's. (The drawing below shows major ore bodies in the Comstock, their dates of discovery, and an indication of the millions of dollars yielded by each.) About the same time, men were growing rich—or richer—from the railroads. The nabobs (wealthy, prominent men) were pleased to have a cable car running up California in the 1870's; it gave them a convenient way to reach the crest of their *hill.*

Riches from Nevada's Mountain of Silver

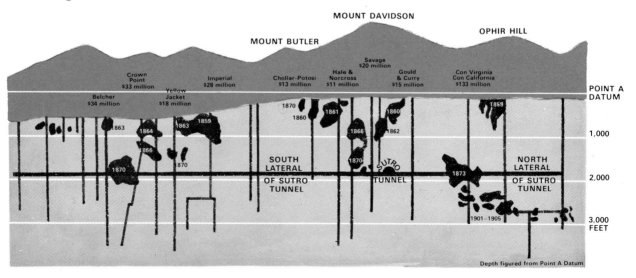

EL DORADO, a rough and ready gambling house of earlier Gold Rush days, was a raucous place with a bar, an orchestra, and a mixed clientele. The city's second big boom—in silver—saw a more refined approach to relaxation for men (see opposite page). Was it a sign of the times . . . or of more money? Probably both.

The Silver Kings

Bonanza—meaning good weather or, for miners, a rich body of ore—is a Spanish word applied to four Irishmen who realized the American Dream.

Before 1867 John W. Mackay and James G. Fair were miners who had been around San Francisco since Gold Rush days. And James C. Flood and William S. O'Brien were bartenders at the Auction Lunch Saloon on Washington Street, who got into the act as mining stockbrokers.

All four men were savvy to tips on the Exchange. When most people figured the Comstock Lode had hit bottom in the late 1860's, these four started buying into, and later owning, the Hale and Norcross Mine. Then they bought control of the California and Consolidated Virginia. And then they announced in the fall of 1873 their greatest strike, the Big Bonanza of western lore.

San Francisco went mining-stock crazy all over again. The "Nevada Four" syndicate waged a financial war with William Ralston and the Bank of California and went on to tie up the Comstock with their control of milling, water, and lumber. In the end, each of the Bonanza Kings had a fortune exceeding $40 million and a personal history that could thrill a Montgomery Street broker even today.

James G. Fair   John W. Mackay   William O'Brien   James C. Flood

...NEVADA SILVER

WATERING HOLE strictly for gentlemen of means, Duncan Nicol's Bank Exchange Saloon was a most proper establishment where the loudest sound heard might be the clearing of a dry throat. Situated on Montgomery Street, Nicol's was handy to the financial center of town.

MAKINGS of a millionaire – the railroads

THE RAILROADS ARRIVE! *East of the Mississippi rail lines had existed for several years prior to 1861, but it wasn't until the outbreak of the Civil War that drawn-out arguments over routes linking the East and the West were brought to a head and work went forward on a transcontinental line. The western portion of the road through the Sierra Nevada was constructed by the Central Pacific Railroad Company (now Southern Pacific), the eastern part by Union Pacific. Guiding powers behind Central Pacific were Charles Crocker, Leland Stanford, Collis P. Huntington, and Mark Hopkins—who came into great fortune through its building and subsequent operation. Although the railroad was much more practical than ships for sending goods from coast to coast, it did not immediately create the miracle boom expected in the far West. Since the western terminus of the line was in Sacramento, there was actually a decrease in business in San Francisco, which was at a disadvantage because of its peninsular location.*

END OF PIONEER WEST was marked on May 10, 1869, by the joining of Central Pacific and Union Pacific rails at Promontory Point, Utah. The classic representation of the ceremonial meeting, at which champagne flowed freely and a symbolic spike of California gold was driven, shows decorous officials of both lines, plus a few gate-crashers. The occasion was originally set for May 9 but was delayed until the next day. Never about to let opportunity pass, San Franciscans began their celebration on the 9th anyway and carried the revelry well into the 11th.

CHARLES CROCKER mansion, above, occupied present site of Grace Cathedral. Crocker was foiled in attempt to obtain adjoining property, owned by a Chinese undertaker, and in a fit of pique built a 40-foot high fence around the owner's house. Huntington home (at right) built by David Colton, friend of Crocker, then purchased by Collis Huntington, stood grandly on what is now Huntington Park.

TURRETED castle at right of picture was built for Mark Hopkins, who employed seven architects. When the Mark Hopkins Hotel was constructed here in 1925, a half-million gallon reservoir was discovered in the courtyard. Site of redwood and marble Stanford home, at left of picture, had a 30-foot stone wall that stretched from California to Pine Street.

The Railroad Kings

Today, memories of the Railroad Kings are stirred by the names of four big buildings in the city—the Mark Hopkins and Huntington Hotels on Nob Hill, the Stanford Court Apartments nearby, and the Crocker-Citizens Bank.

Mark Hopkins, Collis P. Huntington, Leland Stanford, and Charles Crocker were four men who recognized the value of a dollar. They started their careers as storekeepers in Sacramento and parlayed $50,000 into fortunes estimated at $40 to $50 million each. A desperate nation at war during the 1860's had given these shrewd specu-lators an empire in return for a railroad—400-foot right of ways, alternate square-mile sections of public land every ten miles of the track, and bonds to finance the track-laying.

With government subsidies and 15,000 Chinese laborers imported especially for the purpose, the "Big Four" built and raced the Central Pacific Railroad eastward across the Sierra and the Nevada desert. On May 10, 1869, they drove the symbolic golden spike at Promontory Point, Utah, linking the westbound Union Pacific to the Central Pacific.

Charles Crocker

Mark Hopkins

Leland Stanford

Collis P. Huntington

WAS IT the quake, or was it the fire?

DISASTER that struck San Francisco on April 18, 1906, was an earthquake-fire, and historians since seem unable to separate the two events. Union Street (opposite page) was but one of several areas heaved and torn apart by violent earth movements. Lower Market Street (above) suffered quake damage but its greatest destruction was by fire that could not be controlled, owing to broken water mains.

...QUAKE OR FIRE?

HOUSES BUILT ON LOOSE FILL were hit hard by the earthquake; they just seemed to sink down and lean in upon themselves. Four square miles of the city were destroyed in 72 hours. Quake or fire? Both: Twelve city blocks between Van Ness and Polk were relatively undamaged but were dynamited to stop the fire.

OVERTURNED stoves and cracked chimneys started scores of fires after the shaking was over. View of California Street on facing page exemplifies tremendous odds that were finally overcome.

Yesterday, today, and tomorrow are all run together in the exciting blend that is San Francisco. This is neither a city of the past nor of the future, but an intriguing mixture of both—which helps explain why it is such an interesting place today.

PORTRAIT OF AN EXUBERANT CITY

Palace of Fine Arts

Ferry Building

Fisherman's Wharf

FROM TIME TO TIME, nationwide surveys are conducted to determine which American cities make the public pulse beat faster. Usually the results are a revelation to the rest of the United States but seldom are they cause for comment in San Francisco, whose boosters have on occasion been accused of not-so-subtle smugness. To them it is only fitting that San Francisco is invariably rated in the top bracket in terms of beautiful setting, beautiful women, good food, lively night life, and uniqueness.

These are the kinds of words that have been written about San Francisco year after year, but they are the kinds of words that—at least to San Franciscans—never grow stale. San Franciscans know that their home has been lavishly written about, praised to the skies, publicized around the world, yet they believe with a passion that it deserves every good phrase devised about it.

Furthermore, San Franciscans take delight even in less-than-kind words about their city. One early writer described the place in the mid-1800's as a perfect hell where common sense had been thrown aside; a few years later someone else stated that quiet and ease were words without meaning in San Francisco. Rudyard Kipling called it a mad city; writer Neil Morgan has termed it an ingratiating failure (and in the next breath, the most enchanting of all American cities). Because such words ring as true as on the day they were written, they are music to the ears of a native because they only confirm his conviction that San Francisco invites damning with faint praise, which makes it all the more a great place. It little matters to him *what* people think

Chinatown's Grant Avenue

Downtown Flower Stall

Japanese Tea Garden

of his city; the fact that they have thought about it has proved the point of the whole thing—San Francisco is a place that captivates.

Much of San Francisco's captivating quality is a result of its refusal to become stereotyped. Rome is known as the eternal city; Paris is the city of light; Los Angeles is a city on the move. Though it has been given dozens of names, San Francisco defies precise definition and logical description.

Located on the tip of a 32-mile-long, hilly peninsula with a land area of slightly less than 47 miles, San Francisco rises from a site where no planner in his right mind would put a city. Where other cities have been able to spread out, San Francisco has had to climb hills. Where other cities have been able to decentralize their activities, San Francisco has had to concentrate its shopping, its housing, its recreation, its industry. As its residents pridefully point out, the city's physical setting has a lot to do with the way San Francisco is; the relative isolation gives them a feeling of independence.

San Francisco is known for its districts that divide the city into smaller, self-contained cities. Some of them define ethnic neighborhoods, others delineate areas of supposed social distinction. Residents are likely to voice strong feelings about their particular district, but few if any can tell precisely where one neighborhood ends and another begins.

The look of yesterday lives in today's homes.

Georgian brick at 2550 Webster.   *Curved bay windows at 2038 Union.*   *Octagonal gazebo at 2645 Gough.*

A city of paradox

San Franciscans have seldom been known to be bored, what with a fine selection of sophisticated supper clubs and cabaret-theaters where some of the nation's top entertainers hold forth. The Broadway-Columbus region, with its bright lights and raucous noise, is the center of activity for jazz, foreign entertainment, and highly original nighteries where show girls appear on giant swings or dance atop revolving pianos in performances that hark back to the wildest days of the Barbary Coast. There are three public art museums and scores of art galleries throughout the city. In addition to a glittering opera season, San Francisco has its own symphony orchestra and ballet company; legitimate playhouses presenting the best of Broadway; an annual International Film Festival; and an excellent repertory theater company. Sports enthusiasts can watch the big-league variety of baseball, football, and basketball.

A city definitely on the move, San Francisco moves at its own pace and in its own way. There seems never to have been a time in its history when it deliberately set out with any kind of pre-planned notion of where it wanted to go or how it wanted to get there. Whatever San Francisco has become, it got that way in spite of itself—which is one of the countless paradoxes that charm even its most devoted critics.

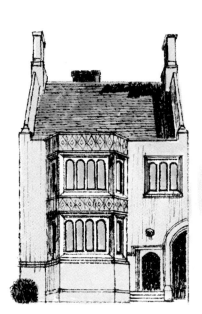

Half-arch for non-existent driveway at 1969 California.

Turrets and towers at 2007 Franklin.

Baroque balconies at 2413-17 Franklin.

WHAT MAKES SAN FRANCISCO WHAT IT IS

Hills, Fog... and People

SAN FRANCISCO IS DIFFERENT. Any resident or visitor knows it, and even people who have never been to San Francisco have convinced themselves—with good reason—that it is a very special place, unlike any other city in the world.

San Francisco owes much of its personality to four endowments: its location, its climate, its topography . . . and its people. Surrounded on three sides by water, the city retains the flavor of special remoteness it had in its earliest days. And with an ocean on one side and an enormous bay on the other, San Francisco's weather is tempered to an almost perpetual spring. "The climate is good for the soul," as one native put it, and ". . . it's why we have so many pretty girls."

The skyline of San Francisco is not just another skyline. Downtown buildings poke up in places where they just shouldn't be, according to logic that applies to other cities. But then San Francisco is a place that defies logic.

IN A CITY OF HILLS, you'll almost inevitably find mesmerized visitors at the most popular overlooks. From their perch atop Twin Peaks, these viewers look down the length of Market Street toward the tall buildings of downtown. Beyond the city, sailboats dot the calm bay. Across the water, East Bay communities spread over the Berkeley-Oakland hills.

A CITY ALMOST surrounded
by water is bound to be different

"THIS PORT OF SAN FRANCISCO . . . is very large, and . . . could hold not only all the armadas of our Catholic Monarch but also all those of Europe," is how Father Juan Crespi described the magnificent bay some two hundred years ago. The Pacific Ocean has strongly influenced the physical form of the Bay Area, and it continues to bear directly on the activities of the people of San Francisco.

...A CITY SURROUNDED BY WATER

WITHOUT WATER on three sides, San Francisco would perhaps be just another city of buildings, streets, and people. Relative inaccessibility has helped make this a place not only conspicuously different but one with a unique personality. The cliff-edge trail at left around Lands End is part of the vast Golden Gate National Recreation Area, which also includes Angel Island (above), a popular destination for cyclists who ferry to the island from Tiburon or San Francisco.

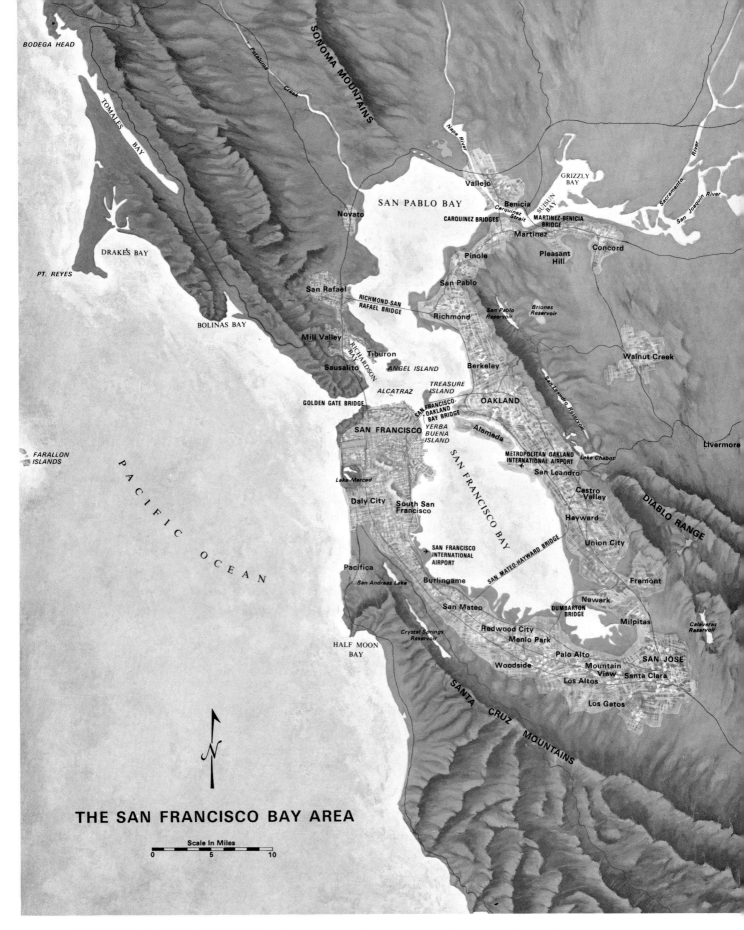

BODEGA HEAD

TOMALES BAY

SONOMA MOUNTAINS

Petaluma Creek

Napa River

DRAKE'S BAY

PT. REYES

Novato

SAN PABLO BAY

Vallejo

GRIZZLY BAY

SUISUN BAY

Sacramento River

San Joaquin River

Benicia

Carquinez Strait

CARQUINEZ BRIDGES

MARTINEZ-BENICIA BRIDGE

Martinez

Concord

BOLINAS BAY

San Rafael

RICHMOND-SAN RAFAEL BRIDGE

Pinole

San Pablo

Pleasant Hill

Richmond

San Pablo Reservoir

Briones Reservoir

Walnut Creek

Mill Valley

RICHARDSON BAY

Tiburon

Berkeley

Sausalito

ANGEL ISLAND

ALCATRAZ

TREASURE ISLAND

OAKLAND

San Leandro Reservoir

GOLDEN GATE BRIDGE

SAN FRANCISCO-OAKLAND BAY BRIDGE

SAN FRANCISCO

YERBA BUENA ISLAND

Alameda

LIVERMORE

FARALLON ISLANDS

Lake Merced

SAN FRANCISCO BAY

METROPOLITAN OAKLAND INTERNATIONAL AIRPORT

Lake Chabot

San Leandro

Castro Valley

DIABLO RANGE

P A C I F I C

Daly City

South San Francisco

Hayward

Union City

O C E A N

SAN FRANCISCO INTERNATIONAL AIRPORT

Pacifica

San Andreas Lake

Burlingame

SAN MATEO-HAYWARD BRIDGE

Fremont

Newark

DUMBARTON BRIDGE

Milpitas

Calaveras Reservoir

San Mateo

HALF MOON BAY

Crystal Springs Reservoir

Redwood City

Menlo Park

Palo Alto

SAN JOSE

Woodside

Mountain View

Santa Clara

Los Altos

SANTA CRUZ MOUNTAINS

Los Gatos

N

THE SAN FRANCISCO BAY AREA

Scale In Miles

0   5   10

GEOLOGISTS CONJECTURE that San Francisco Bay was once a long, rugged coastal depression connected with the Central Valley by a river that flowed out the Golden Gate. One theory says the bay was formed when the sea rose as a result of melting glacial ice.

73

WEATHER REPORT: Fog in morning, clearing by noon

CAPRICIOUS WEATHER is part of San Francisco's charm. Even the seasons refuse to conform to a normal pattern. "Summer" arrives in autumn, and when September heat bears down, natives watch for the cooling fog to billow through the Golden Gate. Many days bring crystal clear air and brilliant sunshine. The wind blows fresh and clean off the sea, ballooning the sails of fast-running craft that skim past the sparkling city.

GOLDEN GATE PARK may be clothed in mist, while other parts of the city are enjoying sunshine and clear skies. Certain neighborhoods pride themselves as being "banana belts," where warm temperatures prevail in little pockets surrounded by chilly, hazy air. In spite of its reputation as a foggy place, San Francisco is one of the nation's three sunniest cities (after Los Angeles and Denver).

ON A WARM DAY, when the air is still and the bay quiet, San Franciscans and visitors flock to the city's outdoor eating places to bask in sunshine and linger long over a last cup of coffee, reluctant to lose one minute of the glorious day.

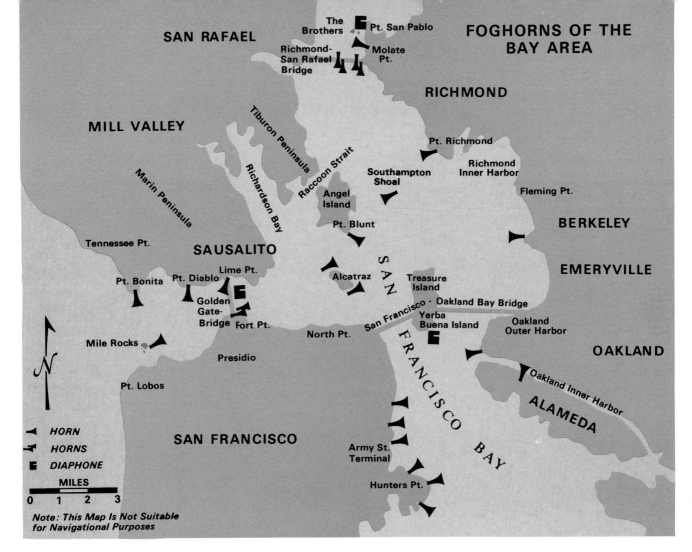

FOGHORNS OF THE BAY AREA

HORN
HORNS
DIAPHONE
MILES
0 1 2 3

Note: This Map Is Not Suitable for Navigational Purposes

LOCATED at key spots around the bay, foghorns (baritone), diaphones (bellow-and-grunt bass), and sirens (soprano) make up a mixed chorus heard most frequently in July, August, September. By listening closely for a minute or two, old-timers can often tell the position of a fog bank by noting which horns are sounding and which are silent. Chart shows the characteristic signals of principal foghorns in the Bay Area.

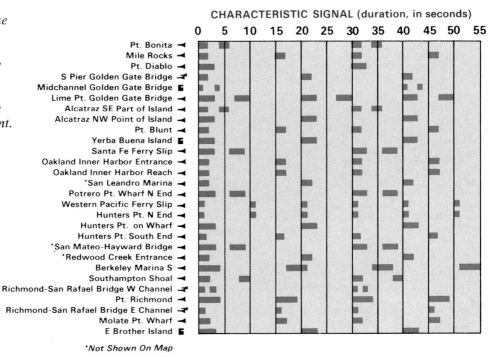

CHARACTERISTIC SIGNAL (duration, in seconds)
0 5 10 15 20 25 30 35 40 45 50 55

Pt. Bonita
Mile Rocks
Pt. Diablo
S Pier Golden Gate Bridge
Midchannel Golden Gate Bridge
Lime Pt. Golden Gate Bridge
Alcatraz SE Part of Island
Alcatraz NW Point of Island
Pt. Blunt
Yerba Buena Island
Santa Fe Ferry Slip
Oakland Inner Harbor Entrance
Oakland Inner Harbor Reach
*San Leandro Marina
Potrero Pt. Wharf N End
Western Pacific Ferry Slip
Hunters Pt. N End
Hunters Pt. on Wharf
Hunters Pt. South End
*San Mateo-Hayward Bridge
*Redwood Creek Entrance
Berkeley Marina S
Southampton Shoal
Richmond-San Rafael Bridge W Channel
Pt. Richmond
Richmond-San Rafael Bridge E Channel
Molate Pt. Wharf
E Brother Island

*Not Shown On Map

A CITY'S CHARACTER is shaped by the variety of its people

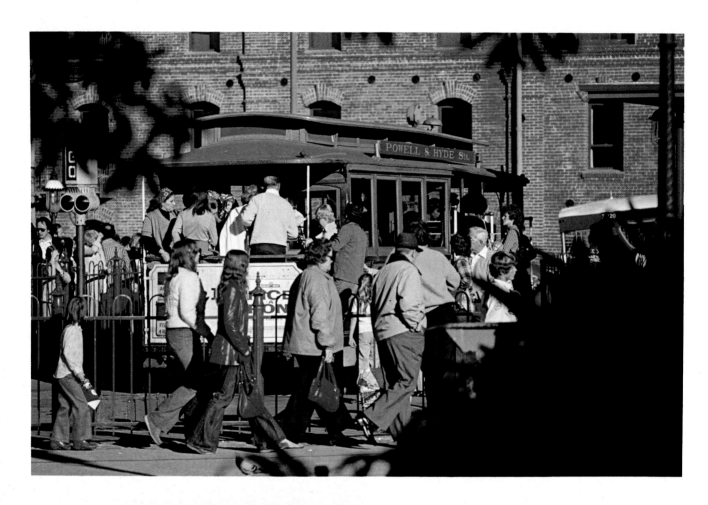

THE CITY'S CHARACTER is best sampled at a busy cable car turnaround. The wide assortment of people lined up to board the cars includes tourist and resident, young and old, bohemian and businessman. Elsewhere in the city, squares and parks play host to a vital cross section of the city comprising roving musicians, self-styled entertainers, and orators. The mixed reactions of their audiences are as fascinating as the shows themselves.

ENTHUSIASM is part of the charm of San Franciscans. It is apparent in the faces of these happy, hill-climbing children and the couple engaged in animated discussion of a craftsman's wares.

WHENEVER THE SUN SHINES, you'll find lunch-time gatherings in the city's parks and plazas. If you want to talk, you can always find someone to talk with, and if you prefer to sit quietly or lose yourself in a good book, no one will disturb you.

*SPONTANEITY is a captivating
quality of San Franciscans. After the initial
thrill of seeing the city's physical charms
has passed, newcomers are struck by the
warmth and open friendliness of San Franciscans.
People notice you, and they talk with you for
no reason other than that they are genuinely
interested in what you have to say. Residents
carry on their daily tasks without becoming so
caught up in them that they can't pause
for a moment to be friendly.*

...THE CITY'S CHARACTER

MOMENTS OF SECLUSION are respected, no matter what the surroundings. In this city a man commands respect whether he wants to pursue "Dear Abby" in Union Square, play a trumpet in Aquatic Park, or, like longshoreman-philosopher Eric Hoffer, read Shakespeare on the waterfront.

THE TOPOGRAPHY consists of hills and more hills

THE HILLS *may be unkind to mailmen, movers, and parked cars, but a hard-breathing scavenger at work on Leavenworth summed up his feelings in a way that speaks for everyone: "These hills are hell to climb, but ain't it great when you get to the top?" Three streets open to automobiles share title as the city's toughest to climb: Filbert between Leavenworth and Hyde; Arguello between Irving and Parnassus; 22nd between Church and Vicksburg.*

FAMILIAR SILHOUETTES *of cable cars crown California Street as the late afternoon sky turns golden and business people scurry home across Nob Hill's blustery summit. The tiny cars, beloved by both visitors and San Franciscans, offer an easy way to surmount some of the city's steepest hills.*

THERE IS NO ONE SAN FRANCISCO

Cities within a City

MORE THAN ONE RESIDENT of San Francisco has been known to have been born, grown up, and died without ever having left his own neighborhood. While such extreme isolationism is rare, there are today many people who leave their neighborhood only during working hours, and then only long enough to go to work. They would not think of going downtown to shop or for entertainment—all this and more is available just a few blocks from home.

Such fierce regional pride is evidenced by such good-natured admissions as, "I wouldn't live anywhere else but out in the Mission," or "Why go downtown—we've got everything we need right here in the Sunset," or "The weather's better, the view is better, everything is better in the Marina." The interesting fact is that such chauvinism is true. Each district, each neighborhood has something all of its own that makes it a place of substance to its residents.

On a relative scale, the people of San Francisco assign more value to places than to things. And because everyone has his own favorite place in the city, it's why there is no one San Francisco.

MAIN ARTERY of Little Italy, Columbus Avenue is touched by extensions of Chinatown and portions of Filipino, Basque, Spanish, and French settlements. Although each culture maintains its personality, the mixture makes for interesting combinations, such as an "Italian" market operated by Chinese, a "Chinese" newsstand run by an Italian.

DOWNTOWN–busy
shopping heart of the city

AT NIGHT THE HEART of San Francisco doesn't just light up—it glows with life. You're looking down from the giddy heights of the Bank of America Building onto Pine Street as it runs eastward toward Market, visible to the right. This is the edge of the city's financial district, a vital part of "downtown" that is filled with hurrying workers by day. At top of photo, the Bay Bridge forms a bright line of lights across the bay.

...DOWNTOWN

A LIVELY SHOPPING AREA spreads outward from Union Square. Colorful flower stands brighten street corners around the square, where brown-baggers from nearby offices and shops bring their lunches on sunny days. To the south, where Powell meets bustling Market Street, tired shoppers rest on benches in sunken Hallidie Plaza.

CITY AND COUNTY OF SAN FRANCISCO

THOUGH RELATIVELY SMALL IN AREA, in comparison with its surroundings—see Bay Area map on page 73—San Francisco occupies a busy, 46½-square-mile peninsula that is the hub of the entire region. From San Jose in the south to San Rafael in the north, and from all over the East Bay, pours a daily flood of humanity that is absorbed chiefly by the city's financial and shopping districts downtown. The downtown area has been called a shopper's mecca in the same sense that London, Paris, and New York are— a world marketplace where anyone can find anything, all within a short walk.

CHINATOWN–principal attraction
for both visitors and natives

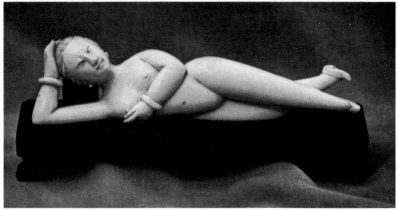

PORCELAIN, cloisonne, jade, and ivory are part of the fun of looking in Chinatown.
Priceless ball at left is actually more than a dozen spheres that have been
painstakingly carved inside one another from a single piece of ivory. Four-inch
ivory lady is helpmate for modest Chinese women who, in describing ailments to doctor,
prefer to point to afflicted area on doll.

POPPING firecrackers and blaring music usher in Chinese New Year, as traditional Golden Dragon is paraded along Grant Avenue during annual celebration that takes place in late February or early March. Visitors escape the crush long enough to admire ivory carvings in a quiet shop.

...CHINATOWN

CHINESE OPERA, held on special occasions, features hours-long performances during which audience drinks tea and socializes to pass the time. Reproductions of classical musical instruments are sold in many Grant Avenue shops.

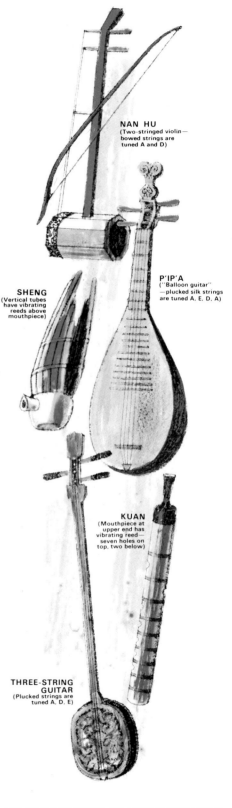

NAN HU
(Two-stringed violin—bowed strings are tuned A and D)

P'IP'A
("Balloon guitar"—plucked silk strings are tuned A, E, D, A)

SHENG
(Vertical tubes have vibrating reeds above mouthpiece)

KUAN
(Mouthpiece at upper end has vibrating reed—seven holes on top, two below)

THREE-STRING GUITAR
(Plucked strings are tuned A, D, E)

FRIVOLITY AND FINE ART are offered by the shops along and off Chinatown's Grant Avenue, but you have to look past the gewgaws to find the gems. Open-air stalls offer everything from thousand-year-old eggs to Wrigley's gum, from authentic temple gongs to picture postcards of the very shops that sell them.

NOB HILL – a history of privilege, a place of prestige

CROWNING NOB HILL, two of the city's venerable landmark hostelries, the Fairmont (above) and the Mark Hopkins (at right), carry on the traditions of dignity and decorum that reach back to the 1800's when the hill was home for San Francisco's most influential families.

FORMER HOME of Comstock millionaire James Flood, the prestigious Pacific Union Club faces California Street just west of Mason. The imposing brownstone was the only Nob Hill mansion to survive the devastating 1906 earthquake.

The Big Men on the Big Hill

The Railroad, Bonanza, and Gold Rush nabobs (slang for wealthy, prominent men) gave Nob Hill its name. The first house on "The Hill of Golden Promise," as it was once called, was built by a Dr. Arthur Hayne in 1856. But not until the cable car was running in the 1870's could people easily reach the crest, and it was then that San Francisco's wealthy moved up the hill.

Richard Tobin built the first mansion, which boasted a tower with a spectacular view in all directions. Then the exodus from fashionable Rincon Hill and South Park began, and Nob Hill became *the* address. Leland Stanford, Mark Hopkins, Charles Crocker, and David Colton—Railroad Barons all—built mansions there. Comstock millionaires like James Fair and James Flood lavished their newly found wealth on building sprees, each trying to outdo the other in gingerbread ornamentation and ornate decoration. Objects of art and special building materials came around the Horn in shiploads. Nob Hill was undeniably gay in the Nineties.

Then came the holocaust of 1906. Everything was leveled except the Flood brownstone, now the home of the Pacific Union Club. A marble portico was all that the fire left of a fine home at Taylor and California Streets. Its pillars now stand in Golden Gate Park, appropriately labeled "Portals of the Past."

Many of the wealthy families didn't rebuild on the same spots. They moved away to join artists and writers on Russian Hill or to build garden homes in Pacific Heights —but always with a view. Where most of the mansions stood on Nob Hill, hotels or huge apartment buildings now rise.

...NOB HILL

NOB HILL offers a delightful surprise in its pocket-sized Huntington Park, a refreshing green oasis sandwiched between the P.U. Club and Grace Cathedral where nursemaids and mothers chat while the youngsters romp in the refined atmosphere.

FOUNTAIN of the turtles, in Huntington Park, was a gift to the city from the Crocker family. The copy of a Roman fountain (by Taddea Landini, 1585) has no turtles, nevertheless it is a pleasant place to discuss an important affair of the moment.

96 AN EXUBERANT CITY

THE TOP OF THE HILL covers about three square blocks. Here, from high above Grace Cathedral, you look east down the length of California Street to the towering buildings of the Financial District. Other streets, such as Taylor in right foreground, drop off steeply to the downtown area.

NEIGHBORHOOD solidarity
near the ocean

IT'S NOT JUST THE WEATHER that stimulates local pride in the Richmond, the Sunset, Parkmerced, and other communities that share the city's western shore. There are brilliant days when the Farallon Islands stand out against the horizon, and there are days when fog billows past 19th Avenue and rests like drifted snow against the sides of Mount Davidson and Mount Sutro but leaves choice areas in islands of sunshine. And 19th Avenue is a case in point of local pride. After World War II the city proposed turning the thoroughfare into a freeway linking Great Highway with Golden Gate Bridge, as part of a master freeway plan. Residents throughout the area rose as one and carried a fierce battle whose repercussions are still being felt.

*HALLMARKS of many neigh-
borhoods west of Twin Peaks
are the living room over the
garage, bay windows facing the
street, a narrow strip of lawn —
and a close, comfortable look.
The surest way to provoke a
resident into a vociferous defense
of the district is to ask him if
he doesn't feel that the area
is a bit cramped.*

...NEAR THE OCEAN

FORTUNATE indeed are San Franciscans who live within sight and sound of the water that virtually encircles the city. Residents of areas such as Sea Cliff (at left) or near Bakers Beach (below) are quite used to the waves that pound just inside the Golden Gate. There is geological evidence in this area that some thousands of years ago the level of the sea was fifty to sixty feet higher than it is now. And the ocean continues to wash at the edges of the city; page opposite shows a stretch of Great Highway where it swings past Fleishhacker Pool and in toward Lake Merced in the southwestern corner of town.

Pistols by the Sea – an Affair of Honor

The period from 1850 to 1860 marked a dueling decade in the raucous life of San Francisco. Duels were frequent and sudden during the Gold Rush, reached a pinnacle of popularity in 1854 and 1855, then were on their way out by 1860.

If a gentleman were insulted, he would follow a strict and formal approach to setting up a duel—the challenge, the acceptance, the selection of a site, the appointment of seconds and surgeons, and the gathering of an audience. By all means an audience! Most duels were well publicized and well attended. An early publication states that the lack of an admission charge seemed the only thing that distinguished the entertainment from bull-and-bear fights. Meadows and glades in the outskirts of the city or near the ocean were the preferred locations. Nearby roadhouses featured early morning "Pistols for two and coffee for one."

It was in a valley near the south shore of Lake Merced that the last duel-to-death took place. State Supreme Court Chief Justice David S. Terry had made insulting remarks about U.S. Senator David C. Broderick. When Broderick heard about them and replied with bitter words, notes were exchanged and the duel was set for September 13, 1859. Broderick's first shot missed, Terry sent a bullet through Broderick's chest, and the Senator died four days later.

THE MARINA – boats, carriage houses, and a view of the Golden Gate

PALACE OF FINE ARTS rises like an ornate bubble near western end of Marina District, whose residents enjoy the city's closest inside view of Golden Gate Bridge as well as the rugged hills of Fort Baker Military Reservation in Marin County.

ON WEEK-ENDS *the yacht harbor is a flurry of activity and the bay is a cloud of sails. Host to one of the most popular pleasure craft harbors in the Bay Area (along with Sausalito and Belvedere), the Marina attracts yachtsmen, Sunday strollers, and picnickers to the Green as well as a flood tide of automobiles along Marina Drive and Lombard Street (Highway 101). Much of the area came into being as a result of land reclamation after the Panama-Pacific International Exposition of 1915.*

Sailboat Watcher's Guide

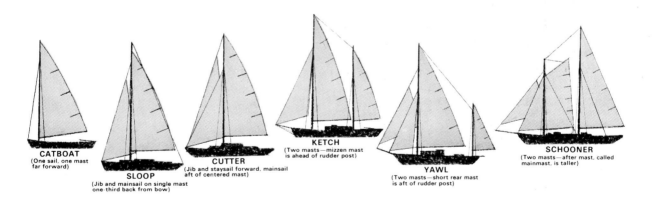

CATBOAT
(One sail, one mast far forward)

SLOOP
(Jib and mainsail on single mast one-third back from bow)

CUTTER
(Jib and staysail forward, mainsail aft of centered mast)

KETCH
(Two masts—mizzen mast is ahead of rudder post)

YAWL
(Two masts—short rear mast is aft of rudder post)

SCHOONER
(Two masts—after mast, called mainmast, is taller)

...THE MARINA

CHRISTMAS season brings traditional chains of lights strung along rigging of boats moored in the harbor. Below, the characteristic architecture of tile roofs and ornate balconies with iron railing is sometimes referred to as Hollywood Mediterranean, and is said to have been inspired during the era of romantic Valentino movies during the thirties.

AN ACTIVE PLACE, Marina Green attracts picnickers, walkers, joggers, sunbathers, volleyball players, bicyclists—and it's a great place to fly a kite. The intriguing piece of fabric at right below does not fly, but plenty of enthusiasm and many helping hands keep it moving.

WALL TO WALL living makes close neighbors

THE HILLS of San Francisco impose some interesting building configurations. Many of the city's fine older homes have breathing space between, even though the sun doesn't reach back too deeply. Entrance is through or past a vertical garden that spills alluvium-like down to the street.

DWELLINGS *that march elbow to elbow across rather than up the hills traverse heights too precipitous for gardens. Such rows are not new to San Francisco, as evidenced in the sketch of Telegraph Hill in the 1870's. When you can't build out and you can't build up, you build close.*

...CLOSE NEIGHBORS

A CITY stacked up on itself (opposite) is the feeling you get when you first see level after level of homes stairstepping up the hills. In the proper light the city looks almost Gothic. In some areas of San Francisco (Sunset, Richmond) wall-to-wall living means a patch of lawn on the streetside and a garden in the rear that encourages back-fence friendships.

QUIET HILLS
south of the slot

A CURIOUS but refreshing place, this region of silent streets is removed from the bustle of downtown, overlooking it almost aloofly. When do Potrero Hill's streets come to life? Where are the people who live here? Who tends the flowers fenced off with a piece of string?

NOT UNCOMMON sights south of Market (an early cable car track gave it the "slot" designation) are a housewife industriously sweeping the sidewalk on Potrero Hill and the sometimes incongruous street names in the Excelsior.

The Short-Lived Montgomery Land Company

In the middle 1860's, astute men of fortune knew that millions were to be made in land as well as in gold and silver. At that time Montgomery Street started at Market and ran north.

South of Market, though, with its Rincon Hill and South Park, was the fashionable heart of the city. So William Ralston, with riches from the Comstock Lode and a 21-year-old millionaire partner, Asbury Harpending, decided to extend Montgomery south to China Basin. They visualized a great tree-lined thoroughfare with parks. The idea was Harpending's, Ralston pledged the backing of his Bank of California, and the two formed the Montgomery Land Company.

The two men eagerly set about acquiring properties. In 1868 they bought key land sections from Market to Howard and put up the 400-room Grand Hotel on the southeast corner of Market.

But, when they attempted to buy property south of Howard to the bay, the landowners, Milton S. Latham and John Parrott of the London and San Francisco Bank, not only refused to sell, but vowed to fight the promoters "every inch of the way." Appeals to the state legislature to condemn the property failed and the Montgomery Land Company was dissolved. Ralston had lost $2,000,000; Harpending's gamble was equally costly. Today, New Montgomery Street extends only two blocks from Market to Howard.

THE MISSION – a mixture of racial backgrounds

"SE HABLA ESPAÑOL," words frequently seen in store windows in the Mission District, reflect the city's Spanish beginnings. Though the Mission is predominantly Latin and though most of the city's Spanish-speaking people live here, they form but part of a blend that includes blacks, Irish, Germans, and Italians. Above, the Mission Neighborhood Association sponsors a street fair in which everyone participates. Cornstalks and family group at right are part of a large outdoor mural by Mujeres Muralistas, three women artists: Graciela Carrillo, Irene Perez, and Patricia Rodriguez. Other murals brighten walls and fences in several Mission District locations.

MISSION DOLORES, established in 1776, was sixth in the California chain. The ornate towers in the photograph at left are part of the Basilica, built in 1916. In the above view from nearby Mission Dolores Park, the high-rises of downtown contrast with bay-windowed Mission District houses.

LOCAL FESTIVALS–everyone is welcome

MUSIC AND GAIETY overflow into streets near Maiden Lane on the opening day of the annual spring flower festival. At right, lamps and a year's happy fortune are sold during the Lantern Festival, one of the highlights of the Chinese New Year celebration.

DAFFODILS and other blossoms bedeck Maiden Lane, and even this horse over a restaurant doorway wears a floral topknot during Maiden Lane's spring festival.

CHERRY BLOSSOM FESTIVAL celebrates many forms of Japanese culture. The master swordsmen below are giving a demonstration of kendo, *an ancient form of fencing practiced by samurai warriors.*

A BOLD PROGRAM of redevelopment

ONCE-DREARY Market Street has undergone a face-lifting. Trees provide welcome shade for shoppers, and some office towers have streetside plazas where flowers, greenery, and the refreshing sound of splashing fountains offer a respite from the surrounding downtown bustle.

A PREPLANNED ADDITION to the city's Financial District, Embarcadero Center features sky-reaching office structures, a hotel, restaurants, shops, and malls. The pedestrian bridge at right connects two buildings of the center.

GOLDEN GATEWAY, a dramatic revitalization of the city's former blighted produce district, invites strolling. Landscaped plazas provide open space between balconied apartment towers and low, white townhouses. Pedestrian bridges link the residential plazas with Sidney G. Walton Square on the north and Embarcadero Center on the south.

...REDEVELOPMENT

FOUNTAINS SPLASH *near many of the city's tall, new buildings. At the foot of Market Street, a spray-washed pathway of concrete squares bridges the fountain pool in Justin Herman Plaza, leading venturesome visitors beneath a labyrinth of tentacles that spout cascades of water. The quieter, dandelionlike fountain at left decorates Maritime Plaza in front of the dramatic, dark-glassed Alcoa Building.*

ARCHITECTURALLY UNIQUE lobby of the Hyatt Regency hotel is a spectacular skylighted atrium rising 17 stories. Ivy cascades from interior balconies. Trees and flower-filled containers brighten the lobby floor, where Charles Perry's 40-foot-high interlacing sphere, Eclipse, floats above a large reflecting pool.

INDIVIDUALITY IN A CULTURAL MELTING POT

A Pride in Ethnic Distinctions

A SIGNIFICANT CLUE to San Francisco's character is the fact that three out of every ten of the Bay Area's inhabitants either were born outside the United States or have at least one parent of foreign stock. The culture of the city has been enriched by the traditions and folkways of many nationalities, many ethnic groups—Chinese, Japanese, Negro, Italian, Greek, and Russian, to name just a few. Most are blended in with the city's residential mainstream, some live in pockets of their own making. If you want to be in Shanghai, visit some of the back alleys in Chinatown off the main tourist thoroughfare. If you prefer Milan or Rome, go to North Beach where the streets that stretch down from Telegraph Hill intersect Columbus Avenue. Tokyo? A few blocks west of Van Ness is Nihonmachi, an area of tiny, old, side-street shops that offer genuine Japanese art objects, and a stretch of modern buildings that offer the newest look in Japanese merchandising.

CONFORMITY is a term infrequently heard and seldom heeded in San Francisco, which has always prided itself on its individuality and on the singularity of its people. Cultural differences in manner, custom, or dress attract little notice.

LITTLE ITALY-a comfortable tie
to the old country

NORTH BEACH: Afternoon sun warming the white fronts of pastry shops and delicatessens
and reflecting off the crosses on the many-spired Church of Saints Peter and Paul. The
Italians have been an influential part of the city since the 1850's, when a finger of the bay
extended between Telegraph and Russian Hills and North Beach was truly a beach.

*THE IDEA of bocce ball is to roll a
wooden ball toward a smaller ball
at the opposite end of a dirt court,
until the two just "kiss" (bocce).
Though the game is chiefly a reason
for afternoon socializing, participants
engage in heated but good natured
argument. A summer's day might also
bring out a varied array of musical
instruments for an impromptu
concert featuring some unorthodox
techniques but favorable results.*

CONVERSATION, high spirits, and good food are much in evidence in the Italian community. No delivery man is expected to merely make his rounds; he must have time to discuss Milan's soccer team or to pass judgment on a pretty girl.

...LITTLE ITALY

THE BUTCHER, THE BAKER . . . . Small family operated shops prepare many of the Beach's local specialties. San Francisco's sea air—so it is claimed—imparts a special flavor and texture to the Italian dry salami and crusty bread.

THE LARGEST Oriental community outside Asia

OTHER FACE of Chinatown is not always apparent to the casual visitor. Cultural identity is preserved in Nam Kue School with instruction in calligraphy, Chinese language, history, and literature. At far right, a helpful kibitzer contributes to Chinese chess game in Portsmouth Plaza ; below, herbalists compound an exotic prescription.

ONE OF MANY formal groups dedicated to helping immigrants cope with unfamiliar surroundings, On Ping Association derives its name from a district in China. Created originally for protection against early prejudice and exploitation, such organizations today have great value in maintaining business and social contacts in the community.

WINTER RAINS MAY MUTE bright colors of Chinatown's streets, but they also help bring out umbrellas in a profusion of pastel shades, as local housewives make their rounds of markets, checking the quality of fresh produce in sidewalk displays.

...ORIENTAL COMMUNITY

TWO CHINESE DELICACIES of high esteem are dried fish—brought to juicy tenderness by steaming—and golden, roast duck, which hangs glistening and dripping in shop windows until cut up for the table. The sight of both is as much a part of the Oriental community as is the blend of exotic smells and sounds in Chinatown's side streets and back alleys.

JAPAN TOWN – new look in the Western Addition

NIHONMACHI *means Japan Town, but it means more than just a multi-block area off Geary, bounded by Laguna and Fillmore. One of the exciting projects of the city's Redevelopment Agency, Nihonmachi furthers Japanese customs and trade in a complex of modern shops and showrooms. Detail at right is from the luxurious Miyako Hotel, which features Japanese-style sunken baths.*

PEACE PAGODA and Plaza are central features in this bit of modern Japan. There are several restaurants serving Japanese foods; showrooms displaying stereo components, television, and automobiles; and shops where you can watch potters at work or classes in classical flower arranging. The spring Cherry Blossom Festival has become an annual event in Japan Town.

YOU CAN TRAVEL the world
without leaving the city

EARLY SOME MORNING, go to one of Chinatown's back alleys, or roam the side streets off Columbus Avenue. Half-close your eyes, sniff the air, and let the sounds flow in and out of your ears, and you'll be in Hong Kong, or Naples.

Headlines of a Rich Racial Potpourri

Your background is Hungarian—or Danish or French or Irish or German or Russian. You want to keep in touch with your heritage but don't feel like an evening at a Japanese theater or a Greek taverna or a Mexican cantina. So you read in any of a score of the city's newspapers about floods in Dublin or credit cards in Zurich or crops in Normandie or medical centers in Stockholm. In San Francisco you may be a newcomer but you're never a foreigner.

NOT EVEN IN FRANCE is French
bread as crusty and as sour as it is in San
Francisco. Loaves ranging from
round to flat to long to very long are sold in hotel
lobbies and at the airport, enabling departing
visitors to take with them a fond memory of the city.
A variety of foods reflecting the tastes of
many nationalities is displayed in shops in
all corners of the city. The imported coffees and
teas below and opposite were photographed
in a gourmet market at the Cannery.

San Francisco's Mixed Background

San Francisco has an international birthright. Six flags (of England, Spain, Mexico, Russia, the Republic of California, and the United States)—flew over the region between 1579 and 1850. The frenzy for gold drew people of all nationalities to the port city. The result was a multiplicity of tongues that often caused unusual misunderstandings.

A trial in nearby San Jose in the 1850's was typical of some of the ways San Francisco had to adjust to its melting pot. A Tartar had been accused of assault by a Spaniard. But proceedings were delayed because the Tartar and his witnesses could not speak English. At last a Tartar named Arghat was discovered who could speak Chinese, and a Chinese named Alab who could speak Spanish. So the trial proceeded in four languages.

With many such adjustments San Francisco has become a city that encourages its immigrants to preserve their cultural identities. The 1960 census ranked Italy first as a source of foreign stock in the city, then Germany and Ireland (followed by the United Kingdom, Canada, Mexico, Russia, Sweden, France, Poland, Austria, and Portugal). However, not long after the 1965 Federal Immigration Law Revision removing restrictions on the entry of Asians to the United States, the city's Chinese population grew to more than 55,000, and the Japanese to more than 11,500. Three distinct cultural communities lie within the city: Chinatown, the largest settlement of its kind outside Asia; North Beach, a "Little Italy" to San Franciscans of Italian extraction; and Nihonmachi, Japan Town, a concentration of Japanese businesses and the site of the $15 million Japanese Cultural and Trade Center.

HOW TO LIVE ON THE TIP OF A PENINSULA

Places People Call Home

SOME SAN FRANCISCANS live in big houses, some in small houses; some live in new houses, some in old houses (others—a good many of them—prefer apartment living). Since the city is a city of hills, many of the dwellings most characteristic of the place sit cozily close to their neighbors. In a city where horizontal space is at a premium, this "wall-to-wall living" may seem crowded but it makes good sense.

Some interesting contrasts are to be found in the places people call home. In areas such as Presidio Terrace or St. Francis Wood, handsome residences sit far back from the street, with lawn areas and gardens surrounding them and separating one from the other. In Presidio Heights or Pacific Heights, many of the structures stand close together but extend in a vertical direction for two or more stories—"one-family homes with two-Cadillac garages," they've been called. In districts such as the Sunset and the Richmond, homes march on for miles, elbow to elbow, back garden to back garden.

Residents of the city's bedroom communities may live fifteen to fifty miles out of the town, nevertheless many of them proudly give their home town as San Francisco.

ROW ON ROW they step up the hillsides, flat fronts and peaked roofs catching the afternoon sun. Land is precious in a city virtually surrounded by water, and houses nestle closely. There is an "at-home" feeling about the bay windows oriented to the last light and the clothes lines stretched over the back yard.

SOME HOUSES
are bigger than others

GRAND MIXTURES of Tudor, Colonial, Renaissance Revival, and San Francisco Riviera characterize splendid areas where the city's social, business, and political leaders reside. The mansions cluster in several distinctive districts—Pacific Heights (whose quiet neighborhood is shown at left), Presidio Heights (opposite page), Sea Cliff, St. Francis Wood, Forest Hill.

"ALONG THE WALL" refers to the western edge of Presidio Heights where it overlooks the fine wooded acres of the presidio. Many of the three-story, one-family houses are shingled and weathered to a deep brown, giving the neighborhood a feeling of substance, a feeling that is certainly not diminished by the front of a Rolls Royce peeking over the wall.

A Window on the World

You can learn a great deal about a city and its residents by observing its windows. Like the people behind them, windows can be carefree . . . or dignified . . . or fussy . . . or spartan . . . or quiet . . . or bold. Size isn't important; personality is. A window, or a city, usually is not special because it's big—it's special because it has a personality all its own.

...BIG HOUSES

DISTINGUISHING FEATURE of many of the city's distinguished homes is a grand gate.
Somehow, a gate is mutely eloquent about the grandeur of the residence that lies beyond.

SURPRISES in a busy metropolis – pockets of urban seclusion

TUCKED AWAY from the casual observer are a wealth of tiny rural spots that would be out of place in any other modern city but seem right in character in San Francisco. The back side of Telegraph Hill is a delightful maze of wooden walks and steep steps overgrown with fern and ivy that—along with the aged houses— make the area look much as it did a couple of generations ago.

HIDDEN FROM THE EYE of everyone except local residents of Russian Hill are tiny lanes where the sun filters through branches or a picket fence to warm a carpet of fallen leaves. Such places are known only to the people who live nearby or to the curious stroller bold enough to push open a sagging gate.

EASTERN SIDE of Telegraph Hill is a mass of jagged rock, painfully bare in many places, but home for cliff hangers. In the early 1900's rock was quarried by casual blasting, so much to the disregard of residents that several houses were brought down or severely damaged until the practice was stopped. San Franciscans like their greenery, whether it covers the house, is confined snugly behind a wall . . . or is cultivated in small containers.

SHARING the view in a city of hills

TIME WAS in San Francisco when hills
were hills and almost everyone who lived on one
could enjoy his favorite view. Now,
with the growth of the city upward, it's not
enough to reside on a hill—you often have to
live in one of the tall buildings in order to see
over another tall building on the next hill.
The drawing below shows comparative heights of
several hills as they would appear squeezed
up close to one another, disregarding relative position.

Do You Look at-or Over-a Hill?

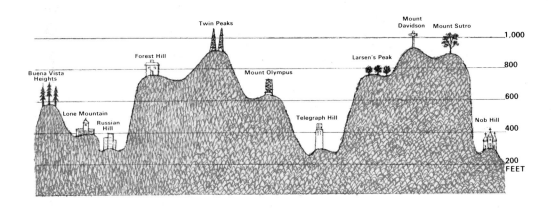

THE PART-TIME San Franciscans –
Where do they come from?

FROM PENINSULA COMMUNITIES and from the East Bay, sleek BART (Bay Area Rapid Transit) trains speed passengers to and from the city over a 75-mile route system that includes subway lines, surface lines, aerial lines, and a 4-mile underwater trans-bay tube.

EVENING TRAFFIC streams over Golden Gate Bridge, carrying Marin residents home or bringing San Franciscans back after a Sunday out of the city. The main link between San Francisco and the north, the bridge experiences traffic jam-ups during peak periods.

EBB AND FLOW of the human tide extends south of the city to the constantly expanding International Airport. A great amount of world traffic moves by air in and out of San Francisco, but perhaps as important to the commerce of the area is the efficient commuter service between the city and Los Angeles.

...PART-TIME SAN FRANCISCANS

GRAND ISOLATION on the unspoiled slopes of Mount Tamalpais in Marin is what some commuters look forward to after a workday in the city. "Tam's" sleeping Indian maiden profile is a familiar sight to the north from San Francisco.

WATER-SIDE communities around the Bay Area are quiet during the work week but come alive with small boats on Saturday and Sunday. Marina living is becoming increasingly popular along the shores from Oakland to Redwood City, from Alameda to Belvedere.

148

A CHILLING FOG envelops Marin commuters as they disembark at the Ferry Building. During commute hours, ferries run between San Francisco and the Marin communities of Sausalito and Tiburon. Many people prefer the relaxing boat trip to the tension-producing drive across the bridge during rush-hour traffic.

A Home Away from Home

The 1860's marked the beginning of the peninsula commute, when building mansions south from San Francisco became fashionable among the wealthy. One of the earliest peninsula commuters, banker William Ralston, made the trip to his suburban estate with his own version of a pony express. The San Francisco and San Jose Railroad line had just been finished in 1864, and Ralston took pride and pleasure in daily races with the train. He frequently won—careening his buggy along the dusty Mission Road at breakneck speed, stopping only at key points for a fresh team of horses.

Ralston built "Belmont," a four-story, eighty-room edifice with banquet hall, ballroom, cut glass doors, silver door knobs and panels, parquet floors, and mahogany-panelled stables. When he died in 1875, his partner William Sharon took over the lavish estate, which is now part of the College of Notre Dame in Belmont.

Financier Darius Ogden Mills selected his homesite in the Buri Buri Rancho, which covered a section of present-day Millbrae and Burlingame. His three-story "Millbrae" had mother-of-pearl and ebony in the master bedrooms and a huge porch overlooking the bay. Apartment houses now stand on the site of Mills' estate.

Probably the most famous peninsula estate known today was Leland Stanford's farm in Palo Alto. It was on his horse farm that Edward Muybridge, father of the motion picture, conducted his photographic experiments. Stanford donated much of his peninsula property to create Stanford University as a memorial to his son.

Nearby in Menlo Park, James C. Flood, of Comstock fame, built what some labeled Flood's wedding cake. "Linden Towers," which stood in what is today called Lindenwood, had three stories topped by a three-story tower, other lesser towers, and elaborate chimneys.

Another banker, John Parrott, selected the Baywood area of San Mateo for a Victorian home, and a retired miner, Alvinza Hayward, built "Hayward Park" nearby, which included a deer and elk preserve as well as a race track. Neither home stands today.

CENTERS OF POWER

Turning the Wheels of Commerce

AN IMPRESSIVE PORTION of world finance is controlled from within the skyscrapers of San Francisco's financial district, and the city is home to four of the nation's 50 largest commercial banks, including the world's largest, The Bank of America. San Francisco is headquarters of the 12th Federal Reserve District, and the Pacific Coast Stock Exchange holds a prominent place among the country's largest regional security markets. Represented in San Francisco are more than 675 insurance carriers, agents, and brokers.

Traditionally the leading world trade center of the western United States and the nation's "Gateway to the Pacific," San Francisco has responded to the needs of the world by making available matchless facilities and a rich fund of economic experience. A great seaport city since the 1800's, San Francisco continues to hold a major position as a cargo port on the West Coast, though a large number of shipping lines now operate out of the Port of Oakland across the bay. Cruise ships embark regularly from San Francisco's piers, heading north to Alaska, south to Mexico, or across the Pacific.

The city's manufacturing base is concentrated in the categories of food processing, apparel and textile products, printing and publishing, and fabricated metal products.

FINANCIAL DISTRICT'S CROSSROADS, California and Montgomery Streets are a beehive of business activity. California is variously known as Insurance Alley and Shippers' Row; Montgomery is called Wall Street of the West and the Street of Banks.

BANKS and brokerage houses – financial strength for the Pacific Coast

ANXIETY and relief, concern and pleasure, mark faces of the men watching the big chalk board at the Pacific Coast Stock Exchange. The Exchange is unique among the nation's securities markets, having one trading floor in San Francisco and another in Los Angeles, 400 miles away, connected by direct voice communication. The time differential between the Atlantic and Pacific seaboards makes this the nation's leading securities market after 12:30 P.M. Pacific Standard Time each market day.

ELOQUENT COMBINATION of massive columns and equally massive automobile on California Street speaks of the stability of the city's financial center. Adjoining Montgomery Street is flanked with banks and brokerage houses, which contribute to the nickname "Wall Street of the West."

The Big Bankers

The golden era of San Francisco banking was actually a silver era. During the Gold Rush—1848 to 1850—almost any storekeeper who had scales and a safe to weigh and store gold dust, was a "banker."

But in 1859, when Nevada's Comstock Lode started to flood California with its silver riches, San Francisco became the financial capital of the West. In 1864, speculators Darius Ogden Mills and William C. Ralston organized the Bank of California and successfully plunged into high-risk mining ventures. William Sharon, "King of the Comstock," cashed in on Comstock madness, the gambling surge for mining shares when stock certificates were hawked on street corners.

Ralston was financing everything from Hunters Point drydocks to South of Market real estate to such edifices as the Grand and Palace Hotels. After the bank failed in 1874, and Ralston swam to his death off North Beach, Sharon and Mills decided to refinance, reorganize, and reopen.

The earthquake and fire of 1906 started the rise of another banking giant, A. P. Giannini. Using his stepfather's vegetable wagon, he rescued and camouflaged the gold resources of his fledgling bank and carted them through the ruins to the safety of his home on the peninsula. Thus his bank, the Bank of Italy (now the Bank of America) was one of the first to honor withdrawals after the conflagration.

William Sharon

Darius Ogden Mills

William C. Ralston

A. P. Giannini

PORT OF CALL for world-oriented shipping

THIS PACIFIC PORT has known days during the Gold Rush when there were so many ships jammed in the bay it was easier to abandon them than to move them, days during World War II that ships headed for the Pacific had to be loaded at anchor because there were not enough docks to accommodate all of them.

155

*HOME BASE for many of the world's
steamship lines and agencies, the Port of San
Francisco shares honors with the Port of
Oakland as a Pacific Coast leader in general
cargo volume, freight, and passenger sailings.
Cruise ship departures are festive occasions.
One of the best places to watch ships glide
under the Golden Gate Bridge is along the
seawall at Fort Point (opposite). When cargo
liners arrive at San Francisco piers, their
freight is ready to move immediately—in
preloaded barges (right) or containers
or in roll-on/roll-off vans and trailers.*

CIVIC CENTER–seat of city and county government

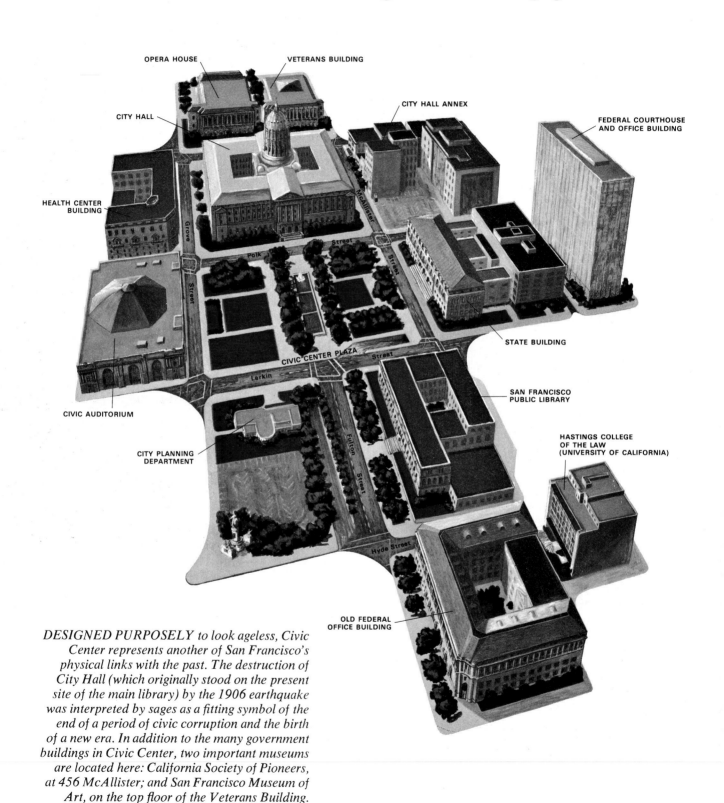

OPERA HOUSE

VETERANS BUILDING

CITY HALL ANNEX

FEDERAL COURTHOUSE
AND OFFICE BUILDING

CITY HALL

HEALTH CENTER
BUILDING

Grove

Polk

Street

Street

McAllister

Street

STATE BUILDING

CIVIC CENTER PLAZA

Street

Larkin

SAN FRANCISCO
PUBLIC LIBRARY

CIVIC AUDITORIUM

Fulton

Street

HASTINGS COLLEGE
OF THE LAW
(UNIVERSITY OF CALIFORNIA)

CITY PLANNING
DEPARTMENT

Hyde Street

OLD FEDERAL
OFFICE BUILDING

DESIGNED PURPOSELY *to look ageless, Civic Center represents another of San Francisco's physical links with the past. The destruction of City Hall (which originally stood on the present site of the main library) by the 1906 earthquake was interpreted by sages as a fitting symbol of the end of a period of civic corruption and the birth of a new era. In addition to the many government buildings in Civic Center, two important museums are located here: California Society of Pioneers, at 456 McAllister; and San Francisco Museum of Art, on the top floor of the Veterans Building.*

CITY HALL is home to the city's board of supervisors, a name normally given to county lawmakers, but applicable to San Francisco's executive body because the city and county are synonymous. The Renaissance architecture is commonly referred to as "classically extravagant," a description that would have delighted James Rolph, Jr., mayor during the period the hall was built. View at right is from Opera House, where in 1945 the United Nations was founded.

CONFIDENTIAL discussion is held on one of the galleries overlooking the vast rotunda in City Hall, a showplace that has seen demonstrations, state funerals, banquets, and a grand celebration of the 63rd anniversary of the 1906 earthquake.

AT DAY'S END, fishing boats bob alongside the Wharf below restaurant row. For thousands who come to the city, a San Francisco visit automatically calls for a meal at Fisherman's Wharf to try such specialties as cracked crab, San Francisco sourdough bread, abalone, and cioppino. The Wharf is a mixture of exciting noises, sights, and smells: crab vendors crying their wares; steam billowing out of cauldrons; the flavor of fresh shrimp; the smell of the sea.

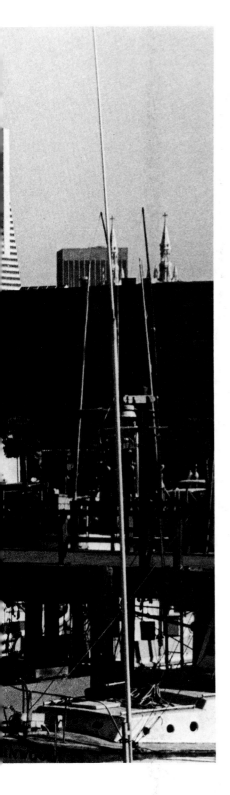

COLLECTING the sea's bounty at the city's doorstep

INTENT on their task of coiling lines and baiting hooks, fishermen prepare for another trip beyond the Gate. Their principal catch will be made up of rockfish.

...THE SEA'S BOUNTY

ALIVE AND KICKING, crabs go straight from the water to retail outlets. Commercial traps (see drawing) are planted on bottom along the surf line, baited with bits of fish. Crabs enter the cages easily but can't get out a wire trapdoor that closes the opening.

How Crabs are Caught

HERE, the farmers still come to town

LITTLE KNOWN except to old-timers and bargain hunters, the city's Farmers' Market is an open-air complex of stalls and walkways where fresh produce from all over the state is available at low prices.

STRAIGHT FROM THE FIELD, melons are unloaded from truck to booth. The retail Farmers' Market, at 100 Alemany Boulevard, just west of the Southern Freeway, should not be confused with the city's wholesale produce district on the east side of the freeway.

FREE SAMPLES and quantity prices. An Old World atmosphere prevails, since most of the growers are Oriental, Portuguese, or Italian, and some good-natured haggling is in order. Many items are available here that are not always readily found in supermarkets, such as savoy cabbage, long Chinese beans, leeks. Apples, obviously, appear in great variety and quantity.

ALL PART OF THE GOOD LIFE

A Special Respect for Culture

THE LUSTY GOLD RUSH ERA was in large part responsible for the development of a cultural background for San Francisco. Though most of the men who streamed into the city by the Golden Gate returned from the diggings poorer than before, each brought a share of his own background or some special talent to a place that was game to try anything. Diversions of the time included multi-lingual musicians, clamorous music halls, and all-male promenade concerts.

As the city grew, women became less a rarity, men who had come into wealth became gentlemen, their ladies became ladies, and discriminating citizens determined that the rough-shod entertainment should at least be tempered with refinement. Several private gambling houses were formed, some saloons became more selective in their clientele, and a process of social selection began.

By the time of the Silver Rush, leading families decided that the good life wasn't just going to happen, and what San Francisco didn't have it wasn't going to sit and wait for. It was a matter of pride that San Francisco should not lag behind in such matters, so with the opening of the transcontinental railroad eastern artists and entertainers were imported in large numbers.

PROPERLY AWED young lady is distracted at a moment that seems to at least visually sum up the city's attitude toward culture. As one writer has said, San Francisco's relationship with the arts has often been stormy . . . there have been quarrels, recriminations, and separations—but there has rarely been indifference.

THE BIG THREE of the art world

FRENCH NOTE is struck at the California Palace of the Legion of Honor, grandly overlooking Lincoln Park and the Golden Gate. A rich repository of Rodin bronzes (The Thinker sits in the courtyard), the Legion contains French antiques and paintings, many paintings of other schools, and the largest collection of drawings and prints in the West.

*FIRST CONTEMPORARY art museum
in the West, San Francisco Museum of
Art is home to magnificent works by
Matisse, Picasso, Braque, Utrillo, and
others. Always in step with the times, the
museum in the War Memorial Veterans
Building in Civic Center hosts exciting
displays of sculpture on a grand scale,
experimental photography exhibits, and
even classic comedy film showings.*

*CITY'S OLDEST MUSEUM, the M. H.
de Young Museum sits in the midst of
pines and eucalyptus in Golden Gate
Park, adjoining the lovely Japanese Tea
Garden. A repository of European and
American art, the de Young houses the
famed Brundage Collection
of jades, Chinese bronzes and
ceramics, and Khmer sculpture.*

PEOPLE-PLEASING FOUNTAIN at Hyatt Hotel on Union Square first attracts passers-by by its cylindrical shape and intriguing texture. A closer look reveals hundreds of tiny figures, like three-dimensional cartoons, depicting scores of city scenes in intimate, amusing, sometimes irreverent detail. Children and friends helped sculptor Ruth Asawa with her work. Figures were shaped from baker's clay, then assembled on 41 large panels from which molds were made for bronze casting.

ONCE-DRAB bank in Mission District is brightened by a 90-foot mural. A group effort, it shows roots, life, and hopes of the Mission District community. Jesus Campusano was the chief designer.

HEROICALLY PROPORTIONED stone sculptures, soaring forms, and brilliant mosaic colors highlight sculptor Beniamino Bufano's artistic legacy to San Francisco. Animals, like this bear and cub, were among his favorite subjects. The tiny (under 5 feet) artist, who died in 1970, attracted almost as much local notoriety for his outspoken criticism of San Francisco art politics as for his massive works.

172 AN EXUBERANT CITY

THE GRAND HOTELS – gold service for visiting royalty

WHERE HORSES ONCE CLATTERED, you now enjoy lunch in an elegant setting. Before the earthquake and fire of 1906, the Garden Court of the Palace Hotel (now Sheraton-Palace) was a palatial carriage courtyard. Today it is a fashionable meeting place for breakfast, lunch, and buffet dinner. Under its high, stained-glass dome have dined presidents, princes, and kings.

...THE GRAND HOTELS

LONG A FOCUS of social pageantry, the St. Francis is a favorite with business people because of its central downtown location. The original St. Francis, built in 1849 at the corner of Dupont (now Grant) and Clay, was termed the fashionable house of the day where the elite of the city boarded or congregated, a description that is as appropriate today as it was then.

"THE MARK" retains the carriage entrance of the old Nob Hill mansion of its namesake, Mark Hopkins. A prime stopping place for visitors, the famous "Top of the Mark" gives a breathless view of the city that is only slightly marred by nearby high-reaching structures.

ORNATE CLOCK is old-time trademark of Nob Hill's other splendid hotel. The Fairmont
is a grand collection of established restaurants and lounges, though some upstarts identify
the hotel's "new" outside elevator overlooking Powell Street as "the thermometer."

WORLDWIDE RESERVATION
service is provided at the
San Francisco Hilton, a modern
hostelry with an open-air
swimming pool on its 16th floor.
Other of the city's grand hotels
include the Clift, whose Redwood
Room is an institution among theater
goers, and the Stanford Court,
built behind the existing façade of the
venerable Stanford Court Apartments.

A RICH VARIETY in the performing arts

SAN FRANCISCO'S history of the theater reaches back to Gold Rush days, when dance halls and saloons featured accordionists and fiddlers to add to the overall merriment. Leading citizens of the time were quick to create a pattern that would polish the rough edges of music hall entertainment and establish a social cohesion to the city's culture, a pattern that has prevailed to this day. At left, a dramatic moment from "Ernani," with Leontyne Price and Renato Cioni; above, a different mood prevails during an agitated scene from "Barber of Seville."

ONE OF LEADING dance groups in the West, San Francisco Ballet enriches the cultural scene of the city with a classical and contemporary repertoire. Though the company has a worldwide itinerary, its open-air performance in Stern Grove is favorite to many devotees. Knowledgeable San Franciscans arrive hours early to watch the rehearsal, equipped with hot coffee to ward off the chill of possible morning fogs.

CLATTERING CASTANETS, clapping hands, and fiery guitar music provide rhythm for the exciting dances of a flamenco group. The Spanish heritage of the city probably has been instrumental in an unabated interest in flamenco long after it faded in popularity in other parts of the country. In addition to performers in clubs, there are several Spanish dance companies in the city.

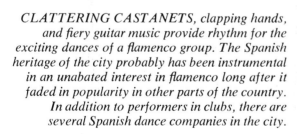

...THE PERFORMING ARTS

EBULLIENT ARTHUR FIEDLER has been conducting members of the San Francisco Symphony in the spirited Pops Concerts since 1950. The mid-summer programs feature promising young artists, many of whom have risen to international fame after their debut with Fiedler. Except for one or two performances at Stern Grove, the concerts are held at Civic Auditorium, where the audience sits at checker-clothed tables on the main floor to enjoy beer and pretzels with their music.

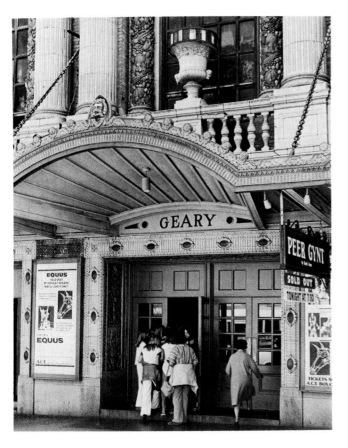

AN ABUNDANCE of theatrical activity is offered by the Curran, Geary, and Marines' Memorial theaters. Pride of the city is the American Conservatory Theater. Since 1967, A.C.T. has been San Francisco's resident professional repertory company. Its theater, the Geary, built in 1910, is included in the National Register of Historic Landmarks.

Men of the Theater

In its Golden Era, San Francisco not only had its Silver Kings and Railroad Kings, but its Theater Kings as well—impresarios who became as famous as the actors and actresses they presented.

The town's first legitimate theater, the Jenny Lind, was in a loft over Tom Maguire's saloon and gambling hall on Kearny Street near Washington. Maguire could neither read nor write, but he was smart enough to know that Gold Rush communities were starved for entertainment.

Countless fires in the ramshackle town often razed the theaters almost as fast as they were built. Between 1850 and 1860 there were three Jenny Linds, two Americans, two Metropolitans, two Adelphis, and a score of other short-lived theaters. In 1876 Maguire went into partnership with Elias (Lucky) Baldwin, the owner of another theater, the Academy of Music. They built the then-fabulous Baldwin Hotel and Theater on Market and Powell Streets. On opening night, at the Baldwin, the assistant stage manager and prompter was a young man named David Belasco, who later achieved fame as a New York producer but who was always known as a San Francisco boy.

There was money in the theater for Henry "Honest Harry" Meiggs too. The same promoter-swindler-alderman who bilked friends and neighbors out of $1 million and built Meiggs Wharf at the foot of Powell near present-day Fisherman's Wharf, also built the large Music Hall on Bush near Montgomery for concerts, oratorios, lectures, and fairs.

AN ORDERLY and civilized social pattern

CLICK OF DOMINOES and clink of coffee cups are the main sounds emanating from the rooms of the city's clubs. In the words of the Chronicle, *clubs offer a haven of privacy in a world in which it is fast disappearing.*

Signs of Select Socializing

Solidarity, selectivity, and status are reflected in the burnished bronze and polished wood signs that represent the world of private clubs. The aims of clubdom, though springing largely from the desire for social contact, vary from epicurian dining to the furtherance of the arts to sports promotion to all-around enjoyment of good times and comfortable surroundings.

GLITTERING *seasonal opening at the War Memorial Opera House brings out many of the city's first families, the proceedings traditionally being attended by members of the press in tails. On facing page, mood of mellowed elegance is mirrored in columns flanking entrance to St. Francis Hotel, one of the more fashionable gathering places downtown.*

The Time and the Place to Play

KEEPING THE NOSE TO THE GRINDSTONE is one thing, but—as San Franciscans believe—wearing the proboscis thin is something else. Never having been a place that takes itself too seriously, San Francisco has a history of enjoying life that dates back to the wild Fourth of July celebration thrown by the town's second settler, when the independence of America was commemorated California style.

A vital part of the enjoyment of life is the enjoyment of good food, and San Francisco has a profusion of good food to delight in. The city's mixed background, plus its adventuresome attitude of being willing to try anything, has done much to give it a varied cuisine, and it has just about everything in the way of good eating that anyone could desire.

San Francisco is often called the city that never sleeps. Though official closing time for night spots is 2 A.M., high spirits stay that way well into the wee hours, and many a party has tapered off with guests taking the morning air at Ocean Beach or in one of the city's many parks.

SAN FRANCISCO—the gayest, lightest-hearted, most pleasure-loving city of the Western Continent, is how writer Will Irwin described the city. Its occasional lapses into seriousness are puckishly tempered, and it enjoys the feeling of being as unfettered as the winds that blow through the Golden Gate.

A CITY full of small parks – for fun, or just relaxing

QUIET RETREATS from the rumble of traffic, the city's many green oases are fine places for lunching or relaxing. The office workers above are enjoying a sunny noontime near the Embarcadero; the picnickers below have found their quiet corner in a little park atop Nob Hill.

CHESS, CHECKERS, or Chinese chess under the pines is a delightful way to spend an afternoon in Portsmouth Plaza. In 1960 the old, run-down park in the plaza was totally excavated for an underground garage, then rebuilt to form a beautifully landscaped place.

SIGMUND STERN GROVE on Sloat Boulevard draws its greatest crowds during summer concert series, especially for the big jazz festival, which features San Francisco's own Turk Murphy and groups large and small from around the Bay Area.

Box Score of San Francisco Parks

Of San Francisco's 46.6 square miles, 3,575 acres are dedicated to parks and recreation centers. Dotting the city as 140 separate breathing spaces, they range in size from the 1017-acre Golden Gate Park and Panhandle to the tiny public gardens with not more than a bench or two. Following are the ten largest, most-used parks in the city:

Name	Principal Use	Location	Acres
Aquatic Park	Fishing	Polk & Beach Streets	31
Fleishhacker Playground	Zoo/Play	Great Highway & Sloat Boulevard	146
Golden Gate Park & Panhandle	General	Ocean Beach to Baker Street	1017
Great Highway/Ocean Beach	Beach	Great Highway Parkway	140
Lake Merced & Harding Park	Fishing/Golf	Skyline & Harding Boulevards	700
Lincoln Park	Museum/Golf	34th Avenue and Clement Street	193
McLaren Park	General	McLaren Park Road	318
Palace of Fine Arts	Open Space	Marina & Lyon Streets	16
Pine Lake Park	Open Space	Crestlake Drive & Vale Street	31
Stern Grove	Concerts	19th Avenue & Sloat Boulevard	33

About 1,050 city acres, including undeveloped land, parks, and other properties, are part of the Golden Gate National Recreation Area. Open spaces also appear in such green spots as Chinatown's Portsmouth Plaza, the city's first plaza, and downtown Union Square. Other green areas include Mission Dolores Park, Washington Park, St. Mary's Square, Balboa Park, Mountain Lake Park, Yacht Harbor, Alta Plaza Park, Bay View Park, Duboce Park, Parkside Square, Huntington Park, Civic Center Plaza, Garfield Square, and numerous recreation centers and playgrounds. Particularly good spots for a view are Buena Vista Hill, Coolbrith Square, Mount Davidson, Fort Funston, Glen Park Canyon, Mount Olympus, Telegraph Hill, Twin Peaks, and Sutro Heights.

...THE SMALL PARKS

A PLACE OF ROLLING HILLS and windswept open spaces, John McLaren Park offers views of the city's northern edge on one side, of Visitacion Valley and the San Bruno Mountains on the other. One of the few city parks in a natural state, its slopes of wild barley and oats surround clusters of eucalyptus, Monterey cypress, and Monterey pine.

EVEN IN FOG, anglers try their luck along the beaches of the Golden Gate National Recreation Area. Some 34,000 acres of land and water—undeveloped coast, state and county parks, military reservations, museums, islands, and privately owned properties—make up this unique area. Its northern boundary is the town of Olema, at the edge of Point Reyes National Seashore; its southern extremity is Fort Funston, at the foot of San Francisco County.

SPACE TO PLAY at the city's edge

*DIVERSE ATTRACTIONS bring
visitors to the headlands of Fort
Funston. Sandy dunes high above the
surf are great hiking grounds.
For some, the land does not offer enough
excitement—they take to the sky
in hang-gliding flights as thrilling
to viewers as to participants.*

*CHILDREN CLAMBER over rocks
at Bakers Beach, where a good ½-mile-long
stretch of sand is an ideal spot for
a family outing. About 1,050 San Francisco
acres are within the boundaries of
the recreation area.*

IN SAN FRANCISCO, celebrating is second nature

ANY TIME is a time to celebrate in the city known for its merrymaking. San Francisco Convention and Visitors Bureau makes available a detailed monthly listing of happy events, among which is the Cable Car Bell Ringing Contest held each August in Union Square.

A GIFT BOX with legs, a flower cart with wheels, and a folk singer with guitar are part of the festivities that occur each March in Maiden Lane to celebrate the arrival of spring. Much of the fun is organized, but most of it is spontaneous and contagious.

A PARTY to start all parties, the Fourth of July bash thrown in 1836 by Jacob Leese (the pueblo's second settler) lasted for two days and a night, beginning San Francisco's legend as the city that never sleeps.

COLORFULLY COSTUMED participants parade for three hours from city hall to Japan Center at the close of the annual Cherry Blossom Festival. Displays and demonstrations at the Japan Center over two weekends present the arts, culture, and beauty of Japan.

HOW TO MAKE the most of a most pleasant leisure

SAN FRANCISCO BAY both links and physically divides the area's cities, which form a unique economic community. The bay moderates the concentration of people; it helps to create a natural air conditioning for San Francisco; it provides water-related recreation facilities. To the people who live on its shores, San Francisco Bay is a body of water to be cherished and protected.

WHEN the stripers are running in the bay (June, July, August), fishermen get there even if it means donning a rubber suit against the icy water. Favorite spots for surf casting are Ocean Beach, Phelan State Beach, Bakers Beach. Inside the Gate there are more rocks to snag a line, but that's little deterrent to anglers at Fort Point, the Marina Green, and Aquatic Park Pier.

WHAT BETTER WAY to spend a lunch break downtown than reading in Zellerbach Plaza. On sunny days office workers relax in the park-like surroundings by listening to occasional concerts or by sitting on "the wall" where they can see and be seen. The stores are an invitation to a little shopping, but when the weather is good there's always tomorrow.

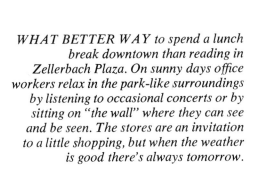

THE TIME TO PLAY   **195**

AFTER DARK, life begins all over again

LIVELY ENOUGH by day, San Francisco becomes increasingly animated with the onset of evening. At Fisherman's Wharf (above), restaurants draw evening crowds, and outside counters do a thriving business in take-home orders of crab, shrimp, and crusty sourdough bread. Ghirardelli Square (below) becomes festive with lights, as shoppers and diners explore an enticing array of shops and restaurants in the old brick structures.

AFTER DARK, Grant Avenue lights up in neon and dragon-entwined street lanterns.
Food markets, furniture shops, and some jewelers close, but restaurants, smaller shops,
and the wax museum welcome visitors for several more hours.

NOT ALL OPERA is at the Opera House, and
not all Greek dancers are in Athens. The Bocce
Ball, an institution in North Beach, features
operatic arias during which the entire
audience occasionally provides a less-professional
yet enthusiastic chorus. Patrons of Greek tavernas
have been known, in their enthusiasm,
to join the costumed dancers.

...AFTER DARK

AFTER the excitement of the early evening has died down, it's time for a breather. A couple shares quiet conversation over Irish coffee behind the tree-framed window of the Buena Vista's back room.

A CONSUMING interest in good food

SAUERBRATEN DAY on Friday fills the great hall of Schroeder's German restaurant on Front Street. Deer heads, coats-of-arms, and steins decorate the dark wood columns.

TEPPAN COOKING is a virtual floor show at Fujiya restaurant in Embarcadero Center. The chef prepares his specialties on a table grill, chopping, mixing, and serving with great style.

Good Food-A Tradition of Variety and Diversity

*International influences have been at work in the city's kitchens
since the days of the Gold Rush when Frenchmen, Chinese, and Germans
flocked ashore from early sailing ships. Over the years the
Italians, Armenians, Basques, Indians, Mexicans, Russians, Spanish,
and Scandinavians have added their contributions. In San Francisco
there is no feeling of affectation when you speak French or Greek or
Japanese to a waiter—it's part of the city's international variety.*

SALT AIR and water-oriented activities

AMID CITYSCAPES and coastal mountains,
San Francisco Bay is an ideal playground for people
with an appetite for salt air and marine
panoramas. Powering out of Sausalito harbor, the ferry
Golden Gate (above) heads for San Francisco. The
city's high-rise skyline is a backdrop for anglers
(left) on one of the many party boats plying the bay.

HE'S SPIED A SANDPIPER hidden in the
marsh. A large part of the value of the bay lies in
its potential as a habitat of fish and wildlife.
The open water, mudflats, and marshlands form
a complex biological system in which living things
exist in a delicate balance created by nature.

ACROSS THE GOLDEN GATE, a swirly, 45-foot dragon kite writhes aloft on a fickle breeze from a bluff at Fort Baker, and cyclists wait to board a San Francisco-bound ferry at Sausalito after a day of leisurely exploring the waterside centers north of the Golden Gate Bridge.

A SATISFIED FISHERMAN admires his catch. This stretch of San Francisco's north waterfront is part of the Golden Gate Promenade, which extends along the water's edge from Fisherman's Wharf to Fort Point. The promenade has retrieved for the public San Francisco's largest bayside beach and the shady clifftop walks of Fort Mason—Army areas that until recently were off limits to civilians.

SECRET OF THE CITY'S CHARM

Creating New Vitality from Old Forms

LET OTHER CITIES tear down the old to make way for the new—let other cities sneer at their adolescence as something to be left behind, something that's better rid of. Though not all residents of the city by the Golden Gate are vitally aware of the place's rich history, most are quick to cry out in protest if a time-worn landmark is in danger of being destroyed in the name of progress.

San Francisco holds its customs and traditions high and fashions its growth to fit them. Hardly a day goes by that the mayor or board of supervisors or planning commission isn't set upon by organized opposition to the destruction of the city's past. A case in point is the Sea Wall, a onetime brick warehouse near the Embarcadero. Doomed, along with several other buildings that were on the site of a new development, the Sea Wall was slated to come down in 1969 under the wrecker's ball. But on the day that demolition was to begin, a group of ladies barricaded themselves in the building, waving banners and shouting slogans. The destruction contractor finally gave in and an agreement was reached whereby that at least the brick façade of the building would be preserved until a decision could be reached on how to affect a permanent preservation of that bit of the past.

OLD BRICK is combined with concrete walkways and open escalators at The Cannery, a revitalized fruit packing plant dating to pre-earthquake days. Arched windows preserve Victorian past in a setting housing ultra-modern shops.

INDIVIDUAL EFFORTS to preserve the character of the past

FEW OTHER CITIES allow themselves to become so enamored of parts of the past that citizens zealously seek out old-time firehouses to be turned into charming dwellings.

DEBATE-PROVOKING point is whether bay windows were originally devised to form a recess in a room or to give a half-circle view of the bay of San Francisco. A house without bay windows is often just another house, but one with them is San Francisco personified.

FRENCH MAILBOX
surmounted by gorgeously crested initials, a large gas lamp, and an ornate door lintel mark the entrance to offices of attorney Melvin Belli on Montgomery Street. Through the doorway is a charming courtyard graced by iron work, plantings, and old brick.

Centers of Restored Elegance

Imaginative renovations have been revitalizing some neglected sectors of San Francisco—most notably the old Barbary Coast, the north waterfront, and Cow Hollow—and transforming them into big business areas as well as prime attractions for visitors and residents alike.

This restoration drama began in 1951 when a group of home furnishing wholesalers bought several dilapidated buildings on Jackson Street's 400-block and set about refurbishing them. Today Jackson Square is a tree-shaded stretch that embraces pockets of the past along adjacent alleys and streets and extends through Pacific Avenue's 500-block.

Another crumbling area had been all but forgotten along the north waterfront. For over a century the multi-level red brick mass at the base of Russian Hill belched smoke and steam, first as a woolen works, later as Domingo Ghirardelli's spice and chocolate factory. Then in 1963 William M. Roth spent $14 million creating Ghirardelli Square, an inviting miscellany of shops, galleries, restaurants, and plazas. The same formula of preservation and renovation inspired Leonard V. Martin to remodel the old Del Monte fruit plant, built in 1894, at Fisherman's Wharf nearby. The Cannery, which began operating in 1967, is now a $7.5 million complex with everything under one enormous roof.

Today's merchants are also doing distinctive things where dairy herds once grazed in the heart of Cow Hollow. Along the 1700- to 2200-block of Union Street, they've turned cowbarns, carriage houses, and Victorian dwellings into a fashionable shopping sector with a charming turn-of-the-century flavor.

*UNION STREET (opposite) is for walkers.
Once part of the city's dairy center, the
street is an intriguing place for exploring
flower-filled courtyards and restored
Victorians that now house delightful shops
and restaurants.*

THE CHOCOLATE FACTORY that became a lively institution

GHIRARDELLI SQUARE, one-time woolen works and later a chocolate factory, is one of the most pleasurable places in the city. Overlooking San Francisco Maritime Historical Park (at left) and Aquatic Park, the miscellany of brick structures bears such captivating names as Mustard Building, Power House, Woolen Mill, Cocoa Building. Of the shops, galleries, theaters, restaurants, and plazas, perhaps the happiest place of all is the old-time ice cream parlor where a limited amount of the rich chocolate is still made in the manner of yesterday and where goggle-eyed children consume sundaes large enough to founder a hungry adult.

TILE ROOFS were not part of the original architectural style, but as elements of new additions they are instrumental in bringing even more warmth to the surroundings. Flower beds, trees, benches, and tables with bright umbrellas all invite visitors to relax and enjoy. The concrete pillars are part of the Ghirardelli bookstore, where browsers crowd each other cozily between well stocked racks. On the level just below the second railing is a close-to-life-sized stone bear with his nose pointing bayward—a creation of Benny Bufano.

*A FOCAL POINT of Ghirardelli Square, the whimsical mermaid fountain designed by
Ruth Asawa is an attraction for youngsters and a favorite meeting place. Beyond the olive
trees is the Wurster Building, named for the architect who remodeled the complex.*

...GHIRARDELLI SQUARE

BENEFACTOR *for this cheerful center was William Roth, a steamship magnate, who feared that if the Ghirardelli buildings were not preserved they would be replaced by a view-spoiling group of high-rise apartments. He bought the place and financed its renovation, preserving the original form but adding to it in similar architectural style. The clock tower houses the studios of a radio station whose call letters are, appropriately, KFOG.*

YOU CAN *take an elevator up, but why ride when the outside stairway between the Cocoa and Mustard Buildings gives such a fine view of the main plaza. Diners are on the terrace of Sea Witch restaurant, which adjoins Portofino Caffe, the place to go in the square if you're in the mood for a cup of very black and very thick espresso.*

THE CANNERY–smart shops
in a setting of old brick

RED BRICK MAZE on Leavenworth, between Fisherman's Wharf and Ghirardelli Square, was a fruit cannery around the turn of the century. Today the cans are gone, and shops and restaurants have brought new vitality to the old property.

SPACES BETWEEN BUILDINGS at The Cannery are as important as the spaces within. The flower filled courtyards are a delight to strollers, who gather to listen to a folk singer or just take their ease in the sunshine. The concourse is shaded by full-sized olive trees, transplanted from northern California, that are strung with tiny lights hardly visible during the day but which make the place a fairyland after dark. The Cannery's star-in-a-circle trademark is taken from the old metal tie plates used in brick wall construction.

THE NORTH WATERFRONT – growing record of a seafaring heritage

BALCLUTHA *sits resignedly at Pier 43 mooring, hard by Fisherman's Wharf and in view of Telegraph Hill, where a semaphore used to notify the town of ships entering the bay. The metal-hulled square-rigger is a floating museum and a colorful reminder of San Francisco's seafaring past.*

"WHAT'S DOWN THERE?" youngsters want to know when they peer through the hatch grating of C. A. Thayer, *an old schooner kept trim and neat at the Hyde Street Pier ship museum.* Thayer *served as a coastal lumber carrier and an Alaskan fishing vessel before sailing to home port in 1957. She's berthed in the company of the scow schooner* Alma, *the steam schooner* Wapama, *and the ferry* Eureka. *It's a quiet retirement for the salt-water veterans.*

THE NORTH WATERFRONT

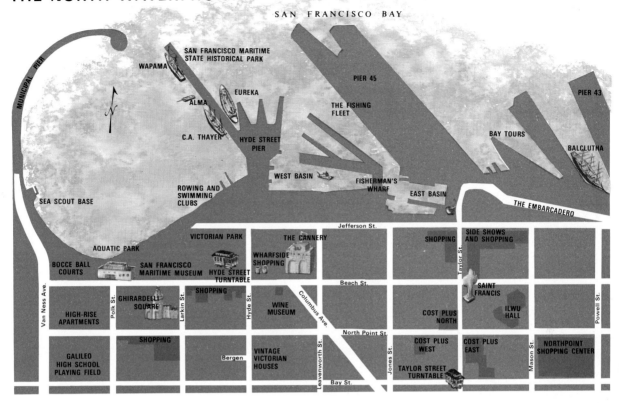

SAN FRANCISCO BAY

MUNICIPAL PIER

WAPAMA

SAN FRANCISCO MARITIME
STATE HISTORICAL PARK

PIER 45

THE FISHING
FLEET

PIER 43

EUREKA

ALMA

BAY TOURS

PIER 43

BALCLUTHA

C.A. THAYER

HYDE STREET
PIER

WEST BASIN

FISHERMAN'S
WHARF

EAST BASIN

ROWING AND
SWIMMING
CLUBS

SEA SCOUT BASE

THE EMBARCADERO

Jefferson St.

VICTORIAN PARK

THE CANNERY

SHOPPING

SIDE SHOWS
AND SHOPPING

AQUATIC PARK

BOCCE BALL
COURTS

SAN FRANCISCO
MARITIME MUSEUM

HYDE STREET
TURNTABLE

WHARFSIDE
SHOPPING

Taylor St.

Beach St.

SAINT
FRANCIS

Van Ness Ave.

HIGH-RISE
APARTMENTS

Polk St.

GHIRARDELLI
SQUARE

Larkin St.

SHOPPING

Hyde St.

WINE
MUSEUM

Columbus Ave.

North Point St.

COST PLUS
NORTH

ILWU
HALL

Powell St.

SHOPPING

GALILEO
HIGH SCHOOL
PLAYING FIELD

Bergen

VINTAGE
VICTORIAN
HOUSES

Leavenworth St.

Bay St.

Jones St.

COST PLUS
WEST

TAYLOR STREET
TURNTABLE

COST PLUS
EAST

Mason St.

NORTHPOINT
SHOPPING CENTER

UNTIL MID-1950, most visitors to the industrial north waterfront came to see the boats at Fisherman's Wharf or to dine in one of the Wharf's seafood restaurants. Today this district contains a growing collection of old sailing vessels that is equaled only at Mystic Seaport, Connecticut; it has one of the country's best maritime museums; and it is a center of major drawing power because of its shopping complexes, theaters, and restaurants.

UNDER FULL SAIL, the Golden Hinde II *sailed into the bay on March 9, 1975, 5½ months after she left England. Now fitted out as a museum, the full-size replica of Sir Francis Drake's famous vessel has a new home at Pier 41. Not far away, at the San Francisco Maritime Museum, beautiful ship models share space with anchors, figureheads, and other objects of maritime lore.*

MONUMENT to "one of the greatest fairs ever"

OPENING OF PANAMA CANAL was celebrated in San Francisco by the Pan Pacific Exposition of 1915 (see below), built on reclaimed land that is today part of the Marina. Twenty-five nations and 43 states and territories contributed to the fair. One of the grandest buildings was the Palace of Fine Arts, designed by Bernard Maybeck to resemble a Roman ruin. The structure on Baker Street was saved from destruction when the rest of the fair was razed, but it crumbled into a genuine ruin over the years. In 1958 local businessman Walter Johnson donated more than $2 million to restore the Palace; this plus other donations and allocations by the city gave San Francisco another permanent landmark.

STROLLING through the magnificent temple is like taking a step into a long-past golden age. Reconstructed at a cost 10 times that of the original, the place now contains a lively science museum that invites you to tinker with the exhibits and make your own discoveries about perception and the laws of the universe. The children at left are intrigued by air currents from a blower cone and upside-down images in the optics exhibit.

THE FORT that guards the Golden Gate

PRESIDIO OF SAN FRANCISCO is a command center for military activities in the eight Far Western states. In its northernmost corner, half-hidden under the Golden Gate Bridge, is Fort Point (officially called Fort Winfield Scott). Built in 1861 along the lines of Fort Sumter, it is a classic example of the brick forts constructed in the 1800's to guard the United States seacoast. During World Wars I and II, German prisoners were housed within its walls and a small gun battery was stationed here. For years the foreboding-looking place was used by the presidio and by other agencies for a storage area and its exterior was known only to fishermen or persons curious enough to find their way down to water's edge under the southern arch of the bridge.

TODAY Fort Point is open to the public daily. From its interior court, visitors can inspect the impressively solid construction. Bricks in the arched galleries were made on Russian Hill and at San Quentin; granite came from China. You can wander freely or take a tour conducted by a knowledgeable guide. Dress warmly for your visit; the winds here are often strong and cold.

LONG HAUL up Hyde Street gives a magnificent view back to the bay, Hyde Street Pier, and Alcatraz. Though they may act blasé about it, San Franciscans are as thrilled as visitors by the hang-on-tight ride on the outside steps of the cars.

A NATIONAL LANDMARK that goes nine miles an hour

SHOWMAN INCARNATE, the gripman keeps up a rapid-fire flow of shouted instructions— ranging from "Hang on for the curve!" to "Step back in the car!" — all accompanied by a personalized rhythm embroidered on the bell. When he hauls back on the grip handle, unwary passengers standing behind are likely to get a solid elbow in the ribs, but it's passed off in good nature. Camaraderie that centers around the cable cars hadn't yet evolved when the picture below was taken of the original Clay Street Line.

...THE CABLE CAR

THAT LITTLE SLOT IN THE STREET has a cable running below it, and that cable can become a nightmare of a snarl if it has to be fished out of the slot. Although the cable and its accompanying hardware are kept under constant surveillance and are carefully maintained, the wire rope on occasion will become frayed or snagged. If the trouble isn't spotted at the powerhouse (located at Washington and Mason), it may require a crew to pry up the cable and repair the damage on the spot. Beauty may be lost on the workmen, but the tracks and switching hardware create unique and interesting patterns in the street.

How a Cable Car Works

San Francisco is the only city in the world with an operating cable car system. And so beloved is it, by both natives and visitors, that in 1964 the U.S. Interior Department's National Park Service declared the cable cars a National Historic Landmark.

Legend has it that Andrew Smith Hallidie, a London-born engineer, was moved to invent the cable system by compassion for the beasts that supplied the power for the old horse cars. The story goes that in 1869 he watched a team of four horses struggling on slippery cobbles to haul a fully laden car up a steep hill. When one horse fell, the car rolled back, dragging all four horses behind it. Hallidie vowed to put a stop to such cruelty and, with his partners, built the Clay Street Railroad Company.

In brief, the mechanical process is as follows: A continuous steel cable, which provides the motive power for all the cars, runs in a slot 18 inches below the surface of the street. This 1¼-inch wire rope travels 840 feet a minute, or about nine miles per hour, and is driven by 12-foot winding wheels turned by an electric motor in the central carbarn.

The connection between the cars and the running cable is a pincer-like device called a grip, which is fastened to the forward truck of

the car and extends down through a slot in the street to the cable. When the gripman pulls the lever back, pressure is put on the cable and the car is put in motion slowly. When he pulls the lever completely back, the car moves forward at nine miles per hour.

Back in 1880 there were eight lines with 112 miles of track criss-crossing the steep hills of San Francisco. Now only 17 miles of track remain, and the total system has been reduced to 39 cars —27 "single-enders" on the two Powell Street routes and 12 "double-enders" on the California Street run. (The single type has turntables at each end of the line, while the double type switches on a "Y" at each end.)

Little has dimmed the popularity of the city's cable cars. Every now and then someone makes suggestions regarding more efficient modes of transportation, but the resulting public clamor can be heard around the world. In 1947 members of a San Francisco citizen's committee resolved to "Save the Cable Cars" and put the issue on a ballot. Save them they did. Now there is a provision in the city charter that guarantees perpetuation of the three remaining lines. And during the peak of the summer season the cable cars continue to carry as many as 25,000 passengers a day.

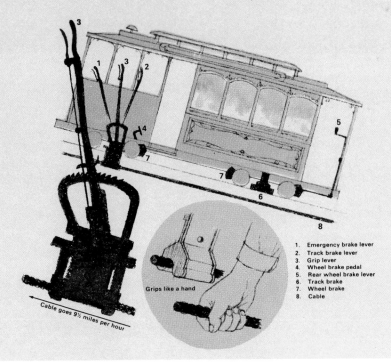

Grips like a hand

Cable goes 9½ miles per hour

1. Emergency brake lever
2. Track brake lever
3. Grip lever
4. Wheel brake pedal
5. Rear wheel brake lever
6. Track brake
7. Wheel brake
8. Cable

STALKING the Victorians – a favorite pastime

PRESERVATION of historic buildings is not unique to San Francisco (New Orleans, Boston, and Philadelphia have protected sectors of old structures), but San Franciscans are unequaled in attachment to their gingerbread palaces. In virtually every district of the city are blocks of Victorians, many of them restored to face-scrubbed newness, most of them proudly occupied by individuals happy to retain this intimate touch with the city's past.

LAGUNA STREET, in its 1800 block, has many homes built between 1885 and 1890 that have been lovingly refurbished by their owners to preserve the early San Francisco flavor. The fronts are a mixture of fine detailing that was the style of the times.

...THE VICTORIANS

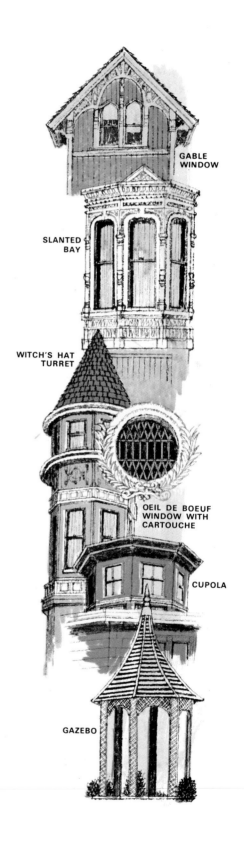

GABLE WINDOW

SLANTED BAY

WITCH'S HAT TURRET

OEIL DE BOEUF WINDOW WITH CARTOUCHE

CUPOLA

GAZEBO

CONTRAST of light and dark so characteristic of San Francisco is epitomized in façades of its old homes (houses above are in 2000 block of Pierce Street). The city's Victorians are characterized by towers, columned porches, wooden filigree, stained glass, and bay windows. Drawing illustrates some of the more common architectural elements.

A Guide to the Victorians

MISSION DISTRICT

Guerrero Street, from 800 block to 1500 block
Italianate, Queen Anne, Stick; several interesting examples of ornate frieze. (In 1886, a Captain A. Dodd ferried lumber for his house, number 1325, to San Francisco aboard his own ship.)

Dolores Street, 700–1500
Stick, Italianate. (In 1879 a Charles Katz purchased number 1202, then a one-room shack; in 1909 he incorporated the original dwelling in a new house built in the Queen Anne tradition.)

Sanchez Street, 300–1700
Stick, Italianate. (Number 775–77, built in 1904 of shingles and wood, is known as the first residence on Sanchez Hill.)

Noe Street, 300–1600
Italianate, Stick—many with ornate detailing. (Numbers 344–46 are good examples of Italianate, while numbers 437–39 are representative of Stick.)

20th, 21st, 22nd, 23rd Streets, 3000–4000
Nearly 40 square blocks containing many fine examples of elaborate Stick, grand Italianate, Queen Anne. (Chemical Company #44 used number 3816 22nd, built in 1910, as its firehouse for over fifty years, when the structure was converted into a residence.)

PACIFIC HEIGHTS

Vallejo Street, 1600–2900
Queen Anne, Stick; some good examples of Baroque Revival and Tudor Revival. (Ephraim Willard Burr, one of San Francisco's early mayors, had number 1772 built as a wedding gift for his son in 1875.)

Broadway, 1700–2900
Good variety of Italianate, Stick, Queen Anne, Colonial Revival, Georgian Revival, Dutch Colonial. (The private school for girls at number 2120 is a former residence of James Flood, the Comstock silver king.)

Pacific Avenue, 1800–3500
Several Queen Anne, several Georgian and Classic Revival, some fine shingled houses.

Jackson Street, 1100–3800
Twenty-seven blocks of Italianate, Queen Anne, Stick; several striking examples of Classic Revival.

Washington Street, 2100–3900
Eighteen blocks of Italianate, Stick, Queen Anne.

Pierce Street, 1900–2700
Queen Anne, Stick, Italianate. (Number 2727 was once the grand manor house of Cow Hollow.)

Scott Street, 1900–3000
Stick, Italianate. (Number 2710 was designed in 1893 by Willis Polk, noted architect around the turn of the century.)

Divisadero Street, 1900–2700
Stick, Italianate; several good examples of turret gable bay windows. (Constructed in 1874, numbers 2229 and 2231 were later purchased and remodeled by Julia Morgan, a San Francisco architect and the designer of William Randolph Hearst's San Simeon.)

RUSSIAN HILL

Green Street, 700–1900
Wide variety of Queen Anne; Italianate apartments; several interesting approaches to shingling.

Vallejo Street, 1000 Block
The only area of frame construction surrounded by the 1906 fire that survived. (Numbers 1013–1015–1017 were the home of the architect Willis Polk.)

Russian Hill Place
Numbers 1, 3, 5, and 7, in the tiled-roof Mediterranean style, were designed in 1915 by Willis Polk.

WESTERN ADDITION

Clay Street, 2400–3900
Wide range of Italianate and Stick; many good examples of Period and Queen Anne detailing. (Number 3362 is a four-story Georgian Revival, designed by Willis Polk in 1896.)

Sacramento Street, 1100–3400
Stick, Italianate; several good examples of French Baroque Revival at numbers 1242 and 2151.

California Street, 1800–3000
Mostly Italianate, with some Stick.

Pine Street, 1800–3000
Wide range of Italianate, Stick. (Three interesting Italianate homes are together at numbers 2018, 2020, and 2022.)

Bush Street, 1600–2900
Good range of Italianate, Queen Anne, Stick; some Classic Revival apartments. (Number 2006, a Victorian Gothic, was built around 1852 and has remained in the same family ever since.)

Sutter Street, 1400–2700
Italianate, Stick; some good examples of Queen Anne. (Number 1815, built in 1878, belonged to Captain and Mrs. John Cavarly, subjects of Kathryn Hulme's *Annie's Captain*.)

Post Street, 1300–2600
Good examples of mixed Queen Anne and Italianate styles (number 1406–08 is one); several flat-fronted Italianates; some Stick.

Laguna Street, 1600–3000
Chiefly Italianate.

Buchanan Street, 1700–2600
Italianate (several fine examples), Stick, Queen Anne. (The handsome brick building at 3640 was headquarters of San Francisco Gas Company.)

Webster Street, 1700–3000
Italianate, Stick, Queen Anne. (Worth noting is the unusual Vedanta Temple at number 2963.)

Steiner Street, 1800–3000
Italianate, Stick; several good examples of Queen Anne.

Baker Street, 1400–2100
Flat-front Italianate, Stick, a few Colonial Revivals. (Numbers 1902, 1905, 1906, 1907, and 1909—all one-story cottages—are said to have been built by the father of Oscar Lewis, noted San Francisco writer.)

Architectural Fashions and Forms

Queen Anne. A style prevailing in England in the 1860's that combines classical designs with medieval, 18th-century, and Japanese motifs; characterized by rounded corner towers, shingles, and combinations of posts or rails with brick or other material.

Stick. A version of Victorian employing structural formulas of Sir Charles Locke Eastlake, English architect; characterized by squared bay windows and ornately decorative brackets.

Italianate. Conforming to style prevalent in Italy from Renaissance to 17th century; characterized by slanted bay windows, fanciful pediments crowning a colonnade, a sense of mass.

Georgian. A distinctive national style prevalent in England in 1702-1830; characterized by deep front or side porches, Palladian windows (arched opening flanked by two smaller, square-headed openings).

THEY SAID IT COULDN'T BE DONE

The Dynamics of Enterprise

THE QUICKEST WAY TO GET RESULTS in San Francisco is to tell a San Franciscan that there is something he is unable to do. This is tantamount to hitting him in the face with a glove, for you have not only thrown out a challenge, you have made it a matter of honor, and the San Franciscan will-by-God do whatever it is you have dared him to do if he has to move the earth to do it.

The city's people like challenges because they are used to them. The earthquake and fire of 1906 posed one of the greatest—that of rebuilding the place after it had been virtually destroyed—and San Franciscans have been taking up the gauntlet ever since.

The city's location itself is a challenge. Being isolated by water on three sides has posed considerable problems. Nature conspires to whittle away the landscape, and not a few answers have had to be found in combatting friendly yet relentless forces of the elements. And no problem ever topped that of connecting San Francisco with the cities and communities across the bay. This challenge was met and conquered in two stages—completion of the Golden Gate Bridge and the Bay Bridge.

GOLDEN GATE BRIDGE was constructed where everyone said a bridge couldn't be built, in the face of enormous opposition that was both natural and man-made. The net slung under the traffic deck between the two towers for the safety of bridge workers is similar to the one used during construction.

GREAT HIGHWAY – at the ocean's edge

PACIFIC COMBERS and vicious current make Ocean Beach a dangerous place to swim, and mist often swirls in over the shore; yet people are forever drawn to the Great Highway that edges the city on the west. For years the city's western shore was constantly being nibbled away by the sea until John McLaren, "father of Golden Gate Park," determinedly compacted brush along much of the beach to keep the sand in place. In later years, concrete piling, extending 13 feet below extreme low tide, stabilized the roadway.

VANTAGE POINT *for viewing a glowing Pacific sunset, Point Lobos at the northern end of Great Highway is lined with cars on a clear evening. At the southern end of the highway, at popular San Francisco Zoological Gardens, animals from the world over roam surroundings similar to their natural habitat.*

WHEN THE TIDE is out the beach is a wide stretch of compacted sand where you can walk almost to the base of Cliff House, perched vulnerably between the ocean and Sutro Heights Park. The latter always seems ready to drop onto the highway despite the artificial stone face given it just to prevent such an occurrence. Cliff House, a gift shop, restaurant, and lounge with a fine view of the ocean, has an incendiary history, having burned several times since its erection in 1863. And when the tide comes in even castles may fall to ruin.

GOLDEN GATE BRIDGE – symbol of a city

"THE GOLDEN GATE is one of nature's perfect pictures—let's not disfigure it," began a notice that appeared in San Francisco newspapers in 1930, campaigning against passage of a six-county bond issue to finance construction of the Golden Gate Bridge. In the face of protracted man-made opposition, and in spite of tides, winds, and fogs that led others to state that it couldn't (or shouldn't) be built, the bridge was constructed and today stands as a monument to one of the most spectacular engineering accomplishments of all time. Though no longer the country's longest single suspension bridge, it is still the most widely recognized symbol of San Francisco. Unique in conception, Golden Gate Bridge is the result of pioneering in law, finance, engineering, and construction.

SAN FRANCISCO ANCHORAGE was designed by Joseph Strauss, chief bridge construction engineer, to spare Fort Point. Except for the high arch over the fort, anchorage at the bridge's Marin end is the same, consisting of three separately poured, massive concrete blocks (see drawing) keyed into one another by their stair-step configuration. Object of the anchorage is to resist cables' pull due to their own weight as well as to bridge load.

How Golden Gate Bridge is Tied Down

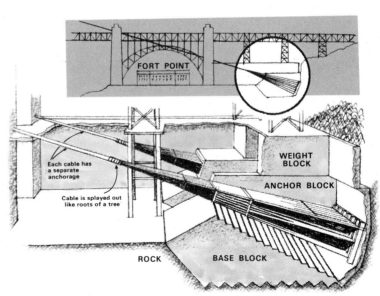

FORT POINT

Each cable has a separate anchorage

Cable is splayed out like roots of a tree

WEIGHT BLOCK

ANCHOR BLOCK

ROCK

BASE BLOCK

...GOLDEN GATE BRIDGE

HEIGHTS are taken in stride by large crew that keeps up a comprehensive, continuous program of inspection and maintenance. Historic photo at left shows bridge half-completed in 1936 at a time when decks reached out in both directions from the two towers.

IT'S FIVE HUNDRED FEET DOWN to the traffic deck (opposite page), 750 feet down to the water. In the distance is the presidio, and beyond that a slightly tipsy horizon, caused by the photographer keeping a firm grip on his perch atop the north tower.

THE BRIDGE that goes through an island

SAN FRANCISCO-OAKLAND BAY BRIDGE and Golden Gate Bridge were completed in
1936-37, and their opening of the city to the east and the north started the end of the bay's
ferry boat era. The Bay Bridge's suspension section and cantilever section (pulled by camera
lens into distorted proximity in photo above) are both double-decked to accommodate a constant
flow of traffic. At north end of Yerba Buena Island is Treasure Island (out of picture to left),
constructed for the Golden Gate International Exposition of 1939-40 and now command
center for U.S. Navy activities in the Pacific Theater.

WEST CROSSING OF Bay Bridge is actually two suspension bridges anchored in the center to a massive concrete pier. Drawing below shows how the Yerba Buena tunnel was "built" first and the hole excavated afterward by boring three pilot tunnels, clearing a channel between them (which served as a partial form for pouring the concrete walls), then blasting the core out. This unusual method eliminated the necessity for shoring up during digging and allowed trucks to back right to the face of the core to haul away excavated rock.

The Hole in Yerba Buena Island

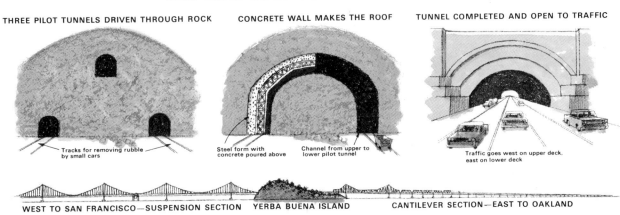

THREE PILOT TUNNELS DRIVEN THROUGH ROCK   CONCRETE WALL MAKES THE ROOF   TUNNEL COMPLETED AND OPEN TO TRAFFIC

Tracks for removing rubble by small cars

Steel form with concrete poured above

Channel from upper to lower pilot tunnel

Traffic goes west on upper deck, east on lower deck

WEST TO SAN FRANCISCO—SUSPENSION SECTION   YERBA BUENA ISLAND   CANTILEVER SECTION—EAST TO OAKLAND

THE BIG PARK that has something for everyone

JAPANESE TEA GARDEN, always a popular Golden Gate Park attraction, is much photographed at cherry blossom time.

GOLDEN GATE PARK, famed as the kind of park every city should have, is a tribute to the vision of William Hall, first park engineer, and the Scottish tenacity of Superintendent "Uncle" John McLaren, who refused to believe that a 3-mile stretch of shifting sand was untamable. The park is entirely man-made, and its variety is indeed impressive. Among its many offerings are sunny meadows (ideal for karate practice), paths through leafy dells, botanical gardens, and 7½ miles of riding trails.

MODEL SAILBOAT enlivens the scene at Spreckels Lake. Both sail and power boat models race here. All of the lakes in the park support resident ducks and migratory waterfowl.

...GOLDEN GATE PARK

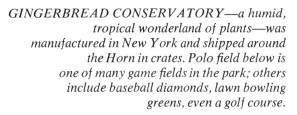

GINGERBREAD CONSERVATORY—a humid, tropical wonderland of plants—was manufactured in New York and shipped around the Horn in crates. Polo field below is one of many game fields in the park; others include baseball diamonds, lawn bowling greens, even a golf course.

BICYCLES AND BOATS transport these park visitors. You can
rent a boat propelled by foot
pump, electric motor, oars, or
paddles. Cycling families enjoyed
the roads in the park before the
coming of the automobile. Today
some roads again belong to
cyclists and walkers on Sundays.

MARKET STREET comes into its own

BUILDINGS OF TODAY dwarf yesterday's skyscrapers. For the fourth time in little over a hundred years, the city's downtown area has undergone a major change, this time in conjunction with the development of a rapid transit system. As always in San Francisco, history has a way of making itself known—during tunneling under Market Street and in the driving of pilings for new downtown buildings, traces of several old ships that were sunk and buried in the 1800's have been discovered. The interpretive drawing below shows the earth's structure in the vicinity of Market Street and the estimated locations of five old vessels whose hulls were covered over by 30 to 50 feet of fill to supply the demand for more building room.

The Ships that Lie Beneath Market Street

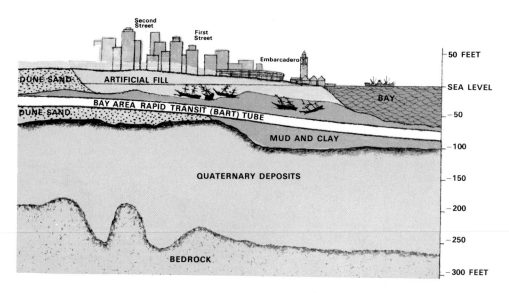

ZELLERBACH PLAZA is a generous, excellently landscaped place that has added a fresh touch to an old thoroughfare. Zellerbach Building, just out of picture to left, was one of the first of contemporary additions to Market Street that gave a new look to the downtown area. The black monolith that rose to an equivalent of twenty stories was at first a startling change to the city's white skyline, but residents soon took pride in a highrise that occupied relatively little airspace.

STANDARD OIL PLAZA is a peaceful garden spot in the busy 300 block of Market Street, a quiet retreat where flowers are constantly in bloom, where shoppers and office workers sit by a sparkling pool during the noon hour.

BART – big link for a network of communities

BAY AREA RAPID TRANSIT system has brought a new dimension in regional travel to San Francisco. Although many eastern cities have had subways for years, undergrounding in San Francisco was long coming. BART is the West's first urban transit system designed specifically to compete with the automobile and hence to reduce congestion from the region's streets and freeways. The system is fully automated. A central computer controls the electrically driven trains, stopping them precisely at boarding points marked on station platforms. But each train has a watchful operator in its cab. Even the fare system is automated: Reusable tickets with magnetically recorded value open the entry turnstiles. At ride's end, the turnstile deducts the fare from the ticket and opens the gate.

BART CAR is a 70-foot-long vehicle seating 72 passengers. It has carpeted floors, wide aisles, recessed lighting, large tinted windows, and automatic air conditioning that adjusts to all temperature variations in the Bay Area. Even the train track is a special design, its gauge being almost a foot wider than standard for better speed and stability. Tracks are mounted on rubber fasteners to give a smoother and quieter ride.

A TUNNEL 150 miles long...full of water

CRYSTAL SPRINGS LAKES (view above is looking south), along with San Andreas Lake, form the storage for San Francisco's water supply. The reservoirs are located in San Mateo County and are situated in the canyons and deep gullies of the San Andreas earthquake fault zone, a natural sink in this area whose valleys have been modified into huge catch basins that trap additional rain water from the surrounding hills.

HETCH HETCHY SUPPLY ROUTE

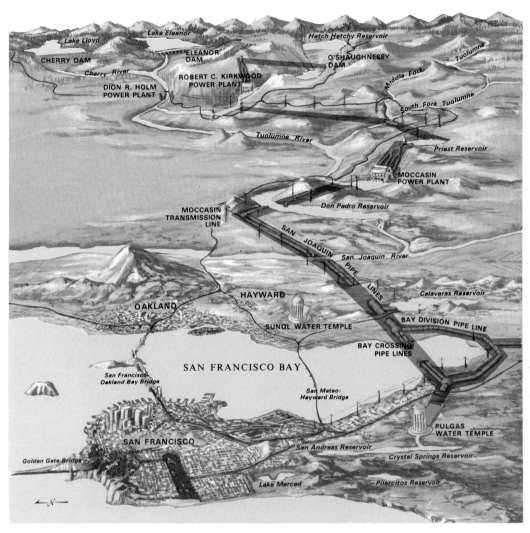

IN EARLY YEARS water was brought to San Francisco from Marin County on rafts, and throughout the latter half of the 1800's local water sources were exploited by private concerns. After bitter struggles with several monopolistic interests, the City and County of San Francisco began construction of the Hetch Hetchy system, which pipes water all the way from the Tuolumne River in Yosemite National Park. Photos above show construction of new pipeline across San Joaquin Valley; a visible stretch of overhead pipe along Edgewood Road in Redwood City; Pulgas Water Temple, off Canada Road west of San Carlos, where the line empties into Crystal Springs Reservoir.

Additional Reading

Books about San Francisco have been considered by writers and publishers to be almost as safe a literary investment as the "Lincoln's doctor's dog" of best-seller tradition. The result is that we find in our libraries almost as many works on the city as there are volumes about Napoleon or George Washington.

And yet it is difficult to compile an ideal reading list of San Franciscana, either for new visitors or for long-time residents.

First, there is the problem of selection. Hasty, mediocre books about San Francisco outnumber volumes of quality; and there is no point in saluting mediocrity here. Second, and more important, American publishers today seem bent on letting their best books go out of print almost before the ink is dry on the pages—or so it seems to both authors and collectors of Western Americana.

It would be futile to list out-of-print books here. In order to secure these uncommon and sometimes rare titles, much time and patience is necessary, as well as the skilled services of a member of the Antiquarian Booksellers Association of America.

A more pleasing development is the trend toward the republishing of minor classics of the past which have been long out of print. They are often presented today in a low-cost paperback format. A second vogue is in the publication of specialized guides to the city, in either hardbound or softbound format. These usually run to regional cuisine, restaurants, and historical architecture, or to guidebooks for urban walking tours.

Luckily for us, some loyal publishers have kept our bookstores stocked with a few of the old favorites, like Oscar Lewis. At the same time, new writers continue to appear, like Doris Muscatine, to sing the praises of the singular city by the Golden Gate. Authors, as a breed, remain about as enchanted with the real San Francisco as they are by the mythical, mystical city of romance.

Visitors and residents alike can profit from this fascination of writing folk with the city. If they will but take the same advantage of San Francisco's bibliography that they do of her other natural resources—her vistas, shops, and bracing climate, to name only three—they will find the delight of their stay, be it 24 hours or 24 years, enhanced by an in-depth knowledge of this storied city on America's sundown shore.

Perhaps the following sampler, compiled by a native son, will be of help.

Richard Dillon

Aidala Thomas. *Great Houses of San Francisco.* New York: Knopf, 1974. $12.95. A spin-off, perhaps, of the Watkins/Junior League volume (below), this is a close view of San Francisco's scrollsaw gothic structures, ornamental details, and so forth. It is illustrated with more than 200 photos by Curt Bruce, all black and white except for a color print of Bardelli's stained-glass peacock.

Asbury, Herbert. *The Barbary Coast.* Sausalito, CA: Comstock Editions, 1973. $1.65 (paperback). The oldest of the exposés of San Francisco's seamy side of life remains the best. A rough-and-tough view of 19th century San Francisco.

Barth, Gunther. *Instant Cities.* New York: Oxford, 1975. $11.95. A scholarly study of the urbanization of the West, with San Francisco compared to Denver. A volume in the *Urban Life in America* series, by a University of California history professor.

Bean, Walton. *Boss Ruef's San Francisco.* Berkeley: University of California, 1952. $2.45 (paperback). A readable, though scholarly, account of the Union Labor Party and city boss Abe Ruef. The latter so corrupted the city that Mother Nature felt it necessary to cleanse the town with an earthquake and fire in April, 1906.

Bear, John. *San Francisco, An Unusual Guide to Unusual Shopping.* Los Angeles: Price, Stern, Sloan, 1972. $3.95 (paperback).

Beebe, Lucius, and Clegg, Charles. *San Francisco's Golden Era.* Berkeley: Howell-North, 1960. $6.95. A fascinating account with rare old woodcuts and other illustrations of the flamboyant side of San Francisco's history, all in the inimitable style of the late Lucius Beebe.

Blakey, Scott, and Hermann, Bernard. *San Francisco.* Papeete, Tahiti: Editions du Pacifique, 1976. $14.95 ($10.95 paperback). A deluxe, color-plate guidebook with text by Blakey and beautiful pictures by Hermann.

Brant, Michelle. *Timeless Walks in San Francisco.* San Francisco: the author, 1975. $3 (paperback). Subtitled "A Historical Walking Guide to the City" and illustrated with some historical photos, this 61-page guide is a pale shadow of Margot Doss's 200-page opus (below).

Bronson, William. *The Earth Shook, The Sky Burned.* Garden City, NY: Doubleday, 1959. $9.95. The definitive history of the 1906 fire and quake is splendidly illustrated with 400 action photos.

Caen, Herb. *One Man's San Francisco.* Garden City, NY: Doubleday, 1976. $6.95. San Francisco's columnar Pepys combs and curries his material in the *Chronicle* to bring out another in his series of light volumes of comment and wit.

Caen, Herb, and Kingman, Dong. *San Francisco, City on Golden Hills.* Garden City, NY: Doubleday, 1967. $12.50. A double-barreled paean to the city. Caen's text is well illustrated by Kingman's sketches, of which 29 are two-tone plates and 41 are color plates; also many black-and-white decorations.

Cameron, Robert. *Above San Francisco.* San Francisco: Cameron, 1969, 1975. Two volumes, each $19.95. Albums of striking aerial photos of San Francisco and the Bay Area.

Chiang Yee. *Silent Traveler in San Francisco.* New York: Norton, 1964. $12.50. Similar to the Caen/Kingman volume, this is an impressionistic view of San Francisco by an Oriental artist, in text and picture; all of the latter are in black and white. The view is refreshing—detached, but sympathetic.

Dickensheet, Dean, Editor. *Great Crimes of San Francisco.* Sausalito, CA: Comstock Editions, 1974. $1.75 (paperback). A collection of true crime tales by David Magee, Oscar Lewis, Lenore Offord, Richard Dillon, Editor Dickensheet, and others.

Dickson, Samuel. *Tales of San Francisco.* Stanford University, 1971. $8.95. Not the most accurate of historians, Sam Dickson was a born storyteller, and his three volumes of yesteryear, *San Francisco Is Your Home, San Francisco Kaleidoscope,* and *The Streets of San Francisco,* appear now in one volume.

Dillon, Richard. *Embarcadero.* Sausalito, CA: Comstock Editions, 1973. $1.50 (paperback). A collection of true stories of adventure on the old San Francisco waterfront during the days of sail.

Dillon, Richard. *The Hatchet Men.* Sausalito, CA: Comstock Editions, 1972. $1.65 (paperback). Still the only full account of the bloody tong wars in Chinatown, when the *boo how doy,* or highbinders, created a reign of terror with hatchets and revolvers.

Doss, Margot Patterson. *Golden Gate Park at Your Feet.* San Francisco: Chronicle Books, 1969. $2.95. A guide to strolls in the city's botanical and horticultural heartland.

Doss, Margot Patterson. *San Francisco At Your Feet.* New York: Grove, 1964. $2.95 (paperback). Subtitled "The Great Walks in a Walker's Town," this is already a minor classic of San Franciscana by the town's most "pedestrious" writer, who shares her favorite walks with all of us.

on San Francisco

Galvin, John, Editor. *First Spanish Entry Into San Francisco Bay*. San Francisco: John Howell, 1971. $7.50. A truly beautiful book of history, well illustrated and finely printed. A collector's item and at a bargain price.

Gentry, Curt. *The Dolphin Guide to San Francisco and the Bay Area*. Garden City, NY: Doubleday, 1969. $1.95 (paperback). A very good *vade mecum* for tourists, especially, since Gentry knows the history as well as the geography of the area.

Gilliam, Harold. *Between the Devil and the Deep Blue Bay*. San Francisco: Chronicle Books, 1969. $2.95 (paperback). Nature writer Gilliam is also the ecological conscience of San Francisco and, particularly, protector of the beautiful—but threatened—bay.

Gilliam, Harold. *The San Francisco Experience*. Garden City, NY: Doubleday, 1972. $6.95. Commentary on the local scene, culled from the author's essays in the *Chronicle*.

Gilliam, Harold. *Weather of the San Francisco Bay Area*. Berkeley: University of California, 1962. $1.85 (paperback). A small, 72-page paperback in the University's *California Natural History Guides* series, explaining the area's curious climate—winds, fogs, and other weather phenomena.

Hansen, Gladys, Editor. *San Francisco, A Guide to the Bay and Its Cities*. New York: Hastings House, 1975. $5.95. A new and revised edition of the classic WPA guide or Federal Writers Project of the 1940's. A volume in the *American Guide Series,* brought up to date by the City Archivist.

Hansen, Gladys. *San Francisco Almanac*. San Francisco: Chronicle Books, 1973. Not quite "Everything You Want to Know About the City," as the subtitle goes, but just about everything—official city flower, the Charter, parks, the town's 43 hills, and more.

Harlan, George. *San Francisco Ferryboats*. Berkeley: Howell-North, 1967. $7.50. The definitive book on the subject, by *the* authority on walking beams and paddle wheels. Illustrated with many fine historical photographs.

Heintz, William F. *San Francisco's Mayors*. Woodside, CA: Gilbert Richards, 1976. $8.95 (paperback). Biographical sketches of some of the city's mayors. Only the chief executives of 1850-80 are covered.

Johnson, Paul C. *San Francisco*. San Francisco: Kodansha, 1974. $2.75 (paperback). A small color-plate guide, with text by the late editor of many *Sunset books*. A bargain in the publisher's *This Beautiful World* series.

Kan, John J., and Leong, Charles. *Eight Immortal Flavors*. Berkeley: Howell-North, 1963. $5.95. More than a cook book, though subtitled "Secrets of Cantonese Cookery," this volume by the much-missed late restaurateur and "Mayor of Chinatown," Johnny Kan, offers insights into the role of cuisine in Chinese culture.

Lavender, David. *Nothing Seemed Impossible*. Palo Alto, CA: American West, 1975. $2.95. A volume in the *Western Biography Series,* this is the story of San Francisco pioneer William C. Ralston.

Levy, Harriet L. *920 O'Farrell Street*. New York: Arno, 1975. $17. A new reprint edition of a charming 1947 reminiscence of comfortable Jewish life in old San Francisco. (The original edition can still be found, for half the price, in large used-book stores, such as Holmes Book Company.)

Lewis, Mary and Richard D. *Where to Go and What to Do With the Kids in San Francisco*. Los Angeles: Price, Stern, Sloan, 1974. $2.95 (paperback).

Lewis, Oscar. *San Francisco: Mission to Metropolis*. Berkeley: Howell-North, 1966. $6.95. The best illustrated history of San Francisco. Lots of pictures and a succinct text by the Dean of San Francisco historians, Oscar Lewis.

The Little Restaurants of San Francisco. San Francisco: Camaro, 1975. $1.95 (paperback). One of many new eating guides, this one specializes in ethnic food in the $1.50-$4.95 price range for meals. Illustrated with pen-and-ink sketches.

Lotchin, Roger W. *San Francisco, 1846-1856*. New York: Oxford, 1974. $12.50. A scholarly view of the city's growing-up years, similar to Barth's in theme. A volume in Oxford University Press's *Urban Life in America* series.

Muscatine, Doris. *Old San Francisco; Biography of a City*. New York: Putnam, 1975. $12.95. This welcome book does not offer a great deal of new information on the city and its history, but it does a masterful job of condensing and combining the work of other writers (Oscar Lewis, Richard Dillon, and others) into one fascinating narrative.

Myrick, David. *San Francisco's Telegraph Hill*. Berkeley: Howell-North, 1972. $9.95. An extra-illustrated (284 historical photos) account of alpine San Francisco by the best local historian to appear since Oscar Lewis.

Palmer, Phil, and Palmer, Mike. *Cable Cars of San Francisco*. Berkeley: Howell-North, 1959. $1 (paperback). A little booklet on the cars, by a father and son team.

Palmer, Phil, and Walls, Jim. *Chinatown*. Berkeley: Howell-North, 1960. $1 (paperback). A much-too-brief view of the Chinese Quarter by photographer Palmer and writer Walls.

Reinhardt, Richard. *Treasure Island*. San Francisco: Scrimshaw, 1973. $12.95. An illustrated memoir—"histalgia" (history/nostalgia)—of "San Francisco's Exposition Years," that is, the good old days before World War II, when the Golden Gate International Exposition preoccupied the city.

San Francisco Bay Guardian, Editor. *San Francisco Free and Easy*. San Francisco: Headlands Press, 1975. $3.85 (paperback). Subtitled "The Natives Handbook," this guide uses the gimmick of being not for tourists but for residents. Certainly it avoids the travel cliches and tourist traps of many guidebooks.

Siefkin, David. *The City at the End of the Rainbow: San Francisco and Its Grand Hotels*. New York: Putnam, 1976. $9.95. A century of the great hotels—Palace, Fairmont, St. Francis, and Mark Hopkins—and their more colorful guests.

Treutlein, Theodore. *Discovery and Colonization of San Francisco Bay*. San Francisco: California Historical Society, 1969. $10. A fine addition to the pioneering studies of George Davidson and Henry Wagner on the discovery and exploration of California's greatest harbor by Fages, Crespi, De Anza, and others.

Walker, Franklin. *San Francisco's Literary Frontier*. Seattle: University of Washington, 1970. $3.95 (paperback). One of the best books ever written about San Francisco, happily back in print again. A splendid survey of 19th century literary life, with emphasis on the 1860's and Twain, Harte, Prentice Mulford, Ina Coolbrith, Charles Warren Stoddard, Henry George, Joaquin Miller, and Ambrose Bierce.

Watkins, Thomas H. *San Francisco in Color*. New York: Hastings House, 1976. $5.95. A reissue of an attractive color-plate guide to San Francisco, a volume in the publisher's *Profiles of America* series. The text is good, but skimpy.

Watkins, Thomas H., and Olmstead, Roger. *Here Today: San Francisco's Architectural Heritage*. San Francisco: Chronicle Books, 1975. $18.95. The inventory resulting from a survey by 200 Junior Leaguers locates historic and esthetic buildings, block by block, with many of them photographed by Morley Baer.

Watkins, Thomas H., and Olmstead, Roger. *Mirror of a Dream: An Illustrated History of San Francisco*. San Francisco: Scrimshaw, 1976. $20. The authors of this extra-illustrated history consider San Francisco to be a clarified reflection of the American dream, a kind of urban Eden which, though damaged, can still be saved.

Index

This book was printed and bound by Graphic Arts Center, Portland, Oregon. Body type is Times Roman, composed by Holmes Typography, Inc., San Jose, California; type for heads is Trooper Roman, composed by Continental Graphics, Los Angeles.